Routledge Revivals

Love Songs of Chandidas

First published in 1967, *Love Songs of Chandidas* provides an informative introduction which makes vividly clear the importance of Chandidas to the Indian peasant masses. As the author tells us, the traveller through the Birbhum area of Bengal hears Chandidas everywhere, in the villages, in the fields, on the roads. Night after night, the people gather in the temple courtyards or on the village greens to listen to professional 'Kirtan' singers sing his songs of the divine love of Radha and Krishna. The influence of Chandidas on contemporary Bengali literature is equally important, his songs having enriched the work of great poets such as Rabindranath Tagore, Govindadas, and many others. The author also discusses the interesting topic of the Sahaja ('spontaneity') movement in Indian faith and literature, as manifested in the songs of Chandidas, and the worship of love-making, divine and human, as an important aspect of this faith. This book will be of interest to students of literature, music, history, cultural studies and South Asian studies.

Love Songs of Chandidas
The Rebel Poet-Priest of Bengal

Translated by Deben Bhattacharya

First published in 1967
By George Allen & Unwin Ltd

This edition first published in 2024 by Routledge
4 Park Square, Milton Park, Abingdon, Oxon, OX14 4RN
and by Routledge
605 Third Avenue, New York, NY 10017

Routledge is an imprint of the Taylor & Francis Group, an informa business

UNESCO Collection of Representative Works Indian Series
This book has been accepted in the Indian Series of the Translations Collection of UNESCO

© UNESCO 1967,1969

All rights reserved. No part of this book may be reprinted or reproduced or utilised in any form or by any electronic, mechanical, or other means, now known or hereafter invented, including photocopying and recording, or in any information storage or retrieval system, without permission in writing from the publishers.

Publisher's Note
The publisher has gone to great lengths to ensure the quality of this reprint but points out that some imperfections in the original copies may be apparent.

Disclaimer
The publisher has made every effort to trace copyright holders and welcomes correspondence from those they have been unable to contact.

A Library of Congress record exists under LCCN: 67112497

ISBN: 978-1-032-76715-4 (hbk)
ISBN: 978-1-003-47979-6 (ebk)
ISBN: 978-1-032-76720-8 (pbk)

Book DOI 10.4324/9781003479796

1. RĀDHĀ AND KRISHNA IN A GROVE

LOVE SONGS OF CHANDIDĀS

The Rebel Poet-Priest of Bengal

TRANSLATED FROM THE ORIGINAL BENGALI
WITH INTRODUCTION AND NOTES
BY
DEBEN BHATTACHARYA

London
GEORGE ALLEN & UNWIN LTD
RUSKIN HOUSE   MUSEUM STREET

FIRST PUBLISHED IN 1967

This book is copyright under the Berne Convention. Apart from any fair dealing for the purposes of private study, research, criticism or review, as permitted under the Copyright Act, 1956, no portion may be reproduced by any process without written permission. Inquiries should be made to the publishers.

© UNESCO, 1967

UNESCO COLLECTION OF REPRESENTATIVE WORKS
INDIAN SERIES
This book
has been accepted
in the Indian Series
of the Translations Collection
of the United Nations
Educational, Scientific and Cultural Organization
(UNESCO)

PRINTED IN GREAT BRITAIN
in 11 *on* 12 *point Old Style*
BY UNWIN BROTHERS LTD
WOKING AND LONDON

ACKNOWLEDGMENTS

I am immensely grateful to Monica Krippner for revising the manuscript and for offering many valuable suggestions during the preparation of this book.

Some of the poems and part of the text of this book were first published in *Encounter*, London; *Vi*, Stockholm; *New India*, New Delhi; *Rajput Painting*, The Gallery, Asia Society, New York, and in *The Loves of Krishna* by W. G. Archer, London, 1957.

FOREWORD

Although a topic of constant speculation, scholarly and otherwise, the life of the poet Chandidās remains an enigma in the literary history of Bengal. Since the fifteenth century his love songs have been of incalculable value to the development of contemporary Bengali literature, and have enriched the works of great poets such as Govindadās, Rabindranath Tagore, and many others.

It is generally agreed that Chandidās lived between the close of the fourteenth century and the first half of the fifteenth,[1] but the exact date of his birth and the facts about his life are uncertain. The only available material from which to construct a probable character of Chandidās are legends, ballads and songs. Though no historical proof exists, either in favour of or against the authenticity of these sources, three important facts concerning his life emerge repeatedly: his apparent connection with the *Sahaja*[2] movement, his career as a village priest, and his relationship with a certain washer-maid named Rāmi, or Rāmini, who lived in his village. Since these facts account for the mood of the songs of Chandidās and the psychological tension which evoked this mood, no other choice remains but to accept this material while attempting to portray the poet.

Because of this lack of recorded history, research work has been made doubly difficult by the emergence of numerous poets who followed in the wake of Chandidās during subsequent centuries, obscuring his identity and causing literary confusion. They assumed his name, his themes and frequently his style. Some added certain prefixes to their adopted name 'Chandidās', using such terms as *Ādi*, meaning the 'first' one; *Badu*, indicat-

[1] *Chandidāser Padāvali*, p. 24, Bimanbihari Mazumdar, Calcutta, 1960, and the essay entitled 'The date of Vidyapati', *Indian Historical Quarterly*, pp. 211–216, 1944, quoted in *Bānglār Bāul O Bāul Gān*, Upendranath Bhattacharya, Calcutta, 1957.

[2] See chapter on the *Sahaja* movement, pp. 44–51.

ing the caste of the poet as Brāhmana,[1] also meaning the 'great' one; *Dwija*, also indicating the caste Brāhmana; *Dīn*, the 'poor' one, and so on. But these prefixes could have been used by the poet himself since he too was a Brāhmana, and at times they were convenient for reasons of poetic metre. Finally, there were other Chandidāses who used no prefix at all.

Two different villages, Chhatna and Nannur in the neighbouring districts of West Bengal, are cited as possible homes of Chandidās. Both these places possess the ruins of an old temple where the poet is said to have been a priest. Chhatna is situated in the district of Bankura and Nannur is in Birbhum, the land of the brave. Nannur is the most favoured as the authentic home of Chandidās.

Out of several thousand songs by various Chandidāses, it has been generally accepted that, on the grounds of language and poetic merit, approximately two hundred are authentic works of the original poet. The majority of the songs translated here are selected from this material. Examples of works signed by Dwija Chandidās and Badu Chandidās are also included.

Chandidās, through his work and life and the legends which surround him, has become a national establishment and must be regarded as such until some miracle of historical research should eventually unravel the tangled data to reveal the real and undisputed facts of his life.

[1] *The caste system:* The Hindu society is a federation of four groups of peoples, identified by their hereditary trades. The *Brāhmanas* represent the intellect or the head of the society; the *Kshatriyas*, the arms or the protecting martial element; the *Vaishyas*, the stomach, representing the merchants who are responsible for feeding the society, and finally, the *Shudras*, the manual labourers, are the legs on which the society stands. These four castes are like vast trade unions, as complex and rigid in their structures as the modern industrial trade unions, but the distinctiveness of the caste system lies in the fact that, in order to maintain a greater efficiency, the trades were restricted to hereditary traditions. Even though the *Brāhmanas* represented the highest caste, they seldom controlled the military or the economic powers. Similarly, the *Vaishyas* with all their wealth seldom achieved the prestige or the respect due to a *Brāhmana* however poor he may have been financially.

CONTENTS

	Page
FOREWORD	
INTRODUCTION	17
Bengali Poetry	27
Rādhā and Krishna	38
The Songs	40
The Sahaja Movement	44

LOVE SONGS OF CHANDIDĀS

1.	*The evening dew*	55
2.	*What sudden sound from the* kadamba *wood*	56
3.	*Who was that girl*	57
4.	*What magic did you play, my love*	58
5.	*Like frozen lightning her fair face*	59
6.	*Danger grew*	60
7.	*Never have I seen such love*	61
8.	*I never touch a black flower*	62
9.	*One day*	63
10.	*I was pouring some water*	64
11.	*Please do not tell me*	65
12.	*You took so long to return*	66
13.	*I throw ashes at all laws*	67
14.	*I harbour in my heart*	68
15.	*I will not treat again*	69
16.	*That terrible love*	70
17.	*I have blackened my golden skin*	71
18.	*One gnawing pain is my home*	72
19.	*This is love*	73
20.	*The more I try to restrain them*	74
21.	*Who can understand*	75
22.	*What god is that*	76
23.	*That son of Nanda*	77
24.	*I took pains in picking the blossoms*	78
25.	*I can walk the way of love*	79
26.	*Disgrace descends on my enchained life*	80
27.	*Who has tampered with your blue skin*	81
28.	*Do not ever throw such insults, my girl*	82

		Page
29.	My poor darling	83
30.	You brought the moon down to my hands	84
31.	Shame fills her world	85
32.	I have hardened my mind	86
33.	Bear the brunt	87
34.	Why did I raise those welcoming flowers	88
35.	My very own man walks away to another's home	89
36.	I can hear the people babbling	90
37.	I want to forget	91
38.	What more can I tell you, my cherished one	92
39.	Do you understand	93
40.	Fear rises and fear returns	94
41.	Not knowing love	95
42.	She lingers out of doors	96
43.	Like lightning in the clouds	97
44.	He was black	98
45.	If, by a great chance, love should ever shoot forth	99
46.	It's no use telling me what I should do	100
47.	What may I call this	101
48.	Whatever the elders at home may say	102
49.	What have I gained	103
50.	My mouth is silent	104
51.	Someone in love can know my feelings	105
52.	Sit yourself down for a while	106
53.	Let us not talk of that fatal flute	107
54.	Has Rādhā pain in her heart	108
55.	Cloud-coloured Kānu, dark mascara	109
56.	The night was dense	110
57.	I must go	111
58.	The morning crows and the kokila cried	112
59.	It's all my fault	113
60.	...Love was the sea of joy	114
61.	With care I combed the earth	115

DWIJA CHANDIDĀS

62.	My growing youth is my one great danger	119
63.	O friend, who made me hear the name of Shyām	120
64.	Consuming me, she moved away	121
65.	...Can anyone follow	122

		Page
66.	*Beloved barefaced one*	123
67.	*Black poison burns me*	124
68.	*. . . My heart can no longer rest*	125
69.	*Enough of this country for me*	126
70.	*Who brought into the world*	127

BADU CHANDIDĀS

71.	*Tell me*	131
72.	*Darkness and clouds*	132
73.	*The cries of the black* kokila	133
74.	*Who play the flute on the Jamunā bank*	134
75.	*I have no idea*	135
76.	*Like the rise of the new sun*	136
77.	*The first watch of the night was a world of a lovely dream*	137
78.	*Krishna*	138
79.	*The rounded* kadambas *in full bloom*	139
80.	*It is in the month of Āsārh*	140

SAHAJA POEMS

81.	*How can I describe*	143
82.	*Using one's body*	144
83.	*They all chatter*	145
84.	*God is the only way*	146
85.	*It is annoying to find*	147
86.	*The changeless land*	148
87.	*Looking deep*	149
88.	*The essence of love*	150
89.	*Kāma*	151
90.	*Mastering Sahaja love is a great art*	152
91.	*One who pervades*	153
92.	*Find your match*	154
93.	*Like the tongue flirting with the tooth*	155
94.	*My body corrodes*	156
95.	*Sun rays*	157
96.	*Away from the contact*	158
97.	*Who could master*	159
98.	*Give up your pride*	160
99.	*Beloved*	161
100.	*Youthful girls*	162

		Page
101.	*There are three categories of men*	163
102.	*All go chattering*	164
103.	*Who can know*	165
104.	*The most difficult of all words*	166
105.	*The essence of beauty*	167

BIBLIOGRAPHY 169

DISCOGRAPHY 170

INDEX 171

ILLUSTRATIONS

1. RĀDHĀ AND KRISHNA IN A GROVE *Frontispiece*
   Kangra, late eighteenth century
   Bharat Kala Bhavan, Benares

2. BIRBHUM LANDSCAPE (17) *facing page* 16

3. NABANI, A BĀUL SINGER FROM BIRBHUM (17) 17
   Photo by courtesy Richard Lannoy

4. NARASIMHA GORING HIRANYAKASHIPU (29) 32
   Illustration of Jayadeva's *Dashāvatāra-stotra*
   Kalighat pat (Bengal folk painting), *c.* 1860
   Victoria and Albert Museum, London

5. VĀMANA QUELLING BALI (29) *between pages* 32–3
   Illustration of Jayadeva's *Dashāvatāra-stotra*
   Kalighat pat, *c.* 1845
   Victoria and Albert Museum, London

6. VISHNU IN THE BODY OF THE BUDDHA (29) 32–3
   Illustration of Jayadeva's *Dashāvatāra-stotra*
   Puri chitrapat (Orissa folk painting), *c.* 1955
   Collection, Deben Bhattacharya

7. HOLI, THE RITE OF SPRING (82) *facing page* 33
   Krishna squirting colour at the cow-girls
   Guler, *c.* 1770, Musée Guimet, Paris

8. RĀGA VASANTA (30) 48
   Krishna dancing with cow-girls while playing a *Vinā* to the spring-time mode Vasanta
   Bundi (Rajasthan), eighteenth century
   Collection, Alan Colquhoun, London
   Photo: John Donat

9. RĀSA MANDALA (31–32) *between pages* 48–9
   Krishna, multiplying himself into many, dances between each pair of cow-girls in a circle
   Mankot, first half of the eighteenth century
   Collection, Raja of Lambagraon

10. RĀSA LĪLĀ (31) 48–9
    The dance of Krishna and the cow-girls, Manipur style

11. BIRTH OF KRISHNA (39) *facing page* 49
    Krishna is being secretly removed to Gokul from the prison of Kamsa, where he was born
    Illustration to the *Bhāgavata Purāna*
    Kangra, 1780–1800, Bharat Kala Bhavan, Benares

12. KRISHNA AT THE BREAST OF HIS FOSTER
    MOTHER, JASHODĀ (39–40)   64
    Kalighat pat (Bengal folk painting), c. 1880
    Victoria and Albert Museum, London

13. KĀLIYA DAMANA—(39 and note 1, p. 96) *between pages* 64–5
    The quelling of the serpent
    Kāliya to protect the cows and the cowherds
    Guler, early nineteenth century
    Punjab Museum, Chandigarh

14. KĀLIYA DAMANA—(39 and note 1, p. 96)   64–5
    The quelling of the serpent Kāliya
    Puri chitrapat (Orissa folk painting), c. 1957
    Collection, Deben Bhattacharya

15. KRISHNA FERRYING THE COW-GIRLS ACROSS
    THE RIVER JAMUNĀ (39)   *facing page* 65
    Puri chitrapat (Orissa folk painting), c. 1955
    Collection, Deben Bhattacharya

16. CHIRA-HARANA (39)   80
    Krishna teasing the cow-girls by stealing their clothes while
    they are relaxing in the river and singing of Krishna
    Kangra, late eighteenth century, Bharat Kala Bhavan, Benares

17. RUKMINI SVAYAMBARAM (27, 39)   *between pages* 80–1
    The marriage of Krishna with Rukmini. Opening scene of the
    Kathakali dance-drama from Kerala

18. RUKMINI SVAYAMBARAM (27, 39)   80–1
    A scene from the Kathakali dance-drama with the Brāhmana
    messenger describing Krishna's charms to Rukmini

19. KĪRTAN SINGING IN BENARES (40)   *facing page* 81

20. KĪRTAN AUDIENCE ON THE STEPS OF THE
    GANGES IN BENARES (40)   96

21. MEETING BY THE RIVERSIDE (59) *between pages* 96–7
    Kangra, early nineteenth century
    Punjab Museum, Chandigarh

22. TOILET OF RĀDHĀ (136)   96–7
    Bundi, eighteenth century
    Ashutosh Museum, Calcutta

23. ABHISĀRIKĀ (74 and note 2, p. 19)   *facing page* 97
    Rādhā, carrying a torch, visits Krishna on a stormy night
    Kangra, nineteenth century, National Museum of India

24. RĀDHĀ AT KRISHNA'S FEET (92)   112
   Kalighat pat (Bengal folk painting), c. 1830
   Victoria and Albert Museum, London

25. HE WAS BLACK, HE HAD POISON-EYES (98)   113
   Bundi (Rajasthan), late eighteenth century
   Municipal Museum, Allahabad

26. KRISHNA SAYING FAREWELL TO RĀDHĀ (111)   128
   Garhwal, c. 1830. Musée Guimet, Paris

27. KRISHNA LEAVING RĀDHĀ IN HASTE FORGETTING HIS SHAWL (112)   129
   Kangra, early nineteenth century. Musée Guimet, Paris

28. RĀDHĀ AND KRISHNA IN EACH OTHER'S CLOTHES (112)   144
   Kangra, 1780–1800
   Collection, Raja of Lambagraon

29. I SCAN DISTANCES IN VAIN (132)   145
   Nurpur, late eighteenth century
   National Museum of India, New Delhi

30. THE FIRST WATCH OF THE NIGHT (137)   160
   Kangra, nineteenth century
   Musée Guimet, Paris

31. THE PASSION-PLAY (150)   161
   Puri chitrapat (Orissa folk painting), c. 1955
   Collection, Deben Bhattacharya

2. BIRBHUM LANDSCAPE (17)

3. NABANI, A BĀUL SINGER FROM BIRBHUM (17)

INTRODUCTION

A journey through the villages of Birbhum in search of the songs of Chandidās, as the translator made, has many compensations. The spring air glitters like dry champagne, throwing into sharp relief the towering heads of the coconut trees and date-palms. Framing the endless paddy fields, bare after the winter harvest, the massive fan-like foliage of the plantain lean against the mango trees. Clusters of clay huts and white-washed brick houses appear to be on fire as the 'crest of Krishna'[1] blazes with savage beauty and the hybiscus explodes into fiery blooms.

In the villages the peasants ceaselessly chatter about their harvests and cows, their families, and about the poet Chandidās. Draped in cotton saris, the women impress the traveller in the same way as their menfolk—they are tough and hardworking, direct and lovable. Sometimes there are Santal villages, lively with chestnut-skinned tribal girls, laughing and gay; or Bengali villages, still and quiet except for the soft cooing of the lazing doves in the mid-day heat. Tobacco smells, blended with the flavours of kitchen spices, hang in the air.

By the roadside singers frequently render, in return for copper coins, Birbhum folk songs, more often than not distorted versions of songs by Chandidās. Chandidās is everywhere—in the villages, in the countryside, even on the roads. As evening falls, the brilliance of the day swiftly fades into soft twilight. Like dew-drops the delicate *bakula* flowers rain down to fill the night air with their gentle fragrance. Spring is always the most eloquent season in Birbhum. The stillness of the country night is regularly broken by the cries for Krishna[2]—the *kīrtan*.[3] Often a temple yard, or the courtyard of a large house, is filled by a spellbound village audience gazing enwrapped at the singers as the tale unfolds. Night after night the people listen to the love songs of Rādhā[4] and Krishna by Chandidās, Dwija Chandidās and many other poets.

[1] Flame-trees.   [2] See Rādhā and Krishna, pp. 38–40.
[3] See The Songs, pp. 40–44.   [4] See Rādhā and Krishna, pp. 38–40.

Some stories give the impression of being the orally circulated history of Chandidās. These were found in a fairly old but undated manuscript and since then they have been discussed and quoted in various works on Bengali literature. For instance, 'He [Chandidās] had seen an image of gold, hidden behind the temple which stood as a pillar of gold, shining in the light of the dawn. That auspicious glance had overwhelmed his heart and he fell at the feet of Bāshuli,[1] asking: "Tell me what I am to do if Rāmi has become of greater importance to me than you? Born into a high-caste Brāhmana family, I worship you with such devotion, yet why should this happen to me?" In reply, as if Chandidās could hear the goddess Bāshuli commanding him: "Conquering the temptation of the senses, you must love this woman. No god can offer you what this woman is able to in terms of the purity of heart".'[2]

But, in the mediaeval Bengali village the scandal of this unconventional liaison gathered force. Chandidās refused to relinquish his duties at the temple, nor would he stay away from Rāmi:

> '...Passion
> opened as a nenuphar[3]
> where the heart's idol dwelt.
> A washer-maid
> fell in love
> with a high-caste priest.
> Words then crawled
> from ear to ear
> and the whole world knew
> of a secret love.
> In the village where they lived,
> they were afloat
> on a sea of blame...'

This beautiful song with its balladic tone is signed by a poet named Chandidās. Judging from the language and the style it seems likely to have been written by a much later Chandidās,

[1] Bāshuli was the deity of the village temple of which Chandidās is said to have been the priest.
[2] Dinesh Chandra Sen quoted in *Chandidās O Vidyāpati*, Shankariprasad Basu, Calcutta, 1960.
[3] White water-lily.

who possibly belonged to the *Sahaja*[1] tradition. In fact, most of the biographical songs which are available today, even though they bear the names of Chandidās and his beloved Rāmi as authors, appear to have been written by village song writers of the seventeenth and eighteenth centuries at the earliest.

These types of folk songs and ballads, legends and quotations from the available literature on Chandidās reveal his life as that of a rebel poet-priest. He had broken tradition by openly living with his great love, the village washer-maid, while still retaining his position as the temple priest of the village. According to the social custom, he was of the highest caste and she of the lowest. A European analogy would be any illicit liaison of a prince of the church. The importance of this liaison is established by the later Chandidāses who went to great lengths to describe the divine nature of this love. Strangely enough, the cause of the *Sahaja* movement appears repeatedly.

The goddess Bāshuli came to the village of Nannur to introduce the *Sahaja* ways. She said to Chandidās, 'You must offer your undivided attention to the practice of the *Sahaja*. Give up the conventional rites of meditation and prayer and devote yourself to being one with Krishna.

'Do as I say along with the *sixty-four*[2] means. Unite your home[3]

---

[1] See The Sahaja Movement, pp. 44–51.

[2] A number of the *Sahaja* songs are written in numerical riddles, presumably to preserve them only for the initiates. The *Sahaja* songs frequently emphasize the fact that all one's faculties must be employed in unison when loving. Therefore, this reference to 'sixty-four' is possibly related to the sixty-four types of *Nayikās*, the women of love, as described in *Rasakalpavalli* of Ramgopal Das, 1673, quoted in *Pānchshata Batsarer Padāvali*, Bimanbihari Mazumdar, Calcutta, 1961. The *Nayikās* are primarily divided into eight categories and then the division is further enlarged into sixty-four. The eight main *Nayikās*, however, represent: *Abhisārikā*, one who, regardless of the weather, goes to meet the lover; *Bāsakasajjā*, one who adorns herself and her home thinking that the lover is bound to come; *Utkanthitā*, the girl who is worried by the absence of her lover; *Vipralabdhā*, one who has already made signs to the lover, but in vain; *Khanditā*, the girl whose love comes to see her bearing the signs of another woman's presence on his person; *Kalahāntarita*, after the quarrel; *Proshitabhartrikā*, the one whose lover has gone abroad; and *Svādhinabhartrikā*, she who has complete control of her lover.

It is also possible that this reference to sixty-four means may represent the sixty-four arts and accomplishments that a lover should study and achieve in order to reach a superior standard in love-making. These involve practically all the imaginable arts and sciences. For a detailed description consult *Kāmasutra* by *Vātsyāyana*.

[3] *Griha:* literally the house, or the home. It is used here in the sense of the physical body, also representing the divine masculine power.

and the earth[1] with the passion-arrows of the god of love. This is the eternal prayer in the *Sahaja* way...

'The woman you love, you must not possess. Rāmini, the washer-maid, represents Rādhā herself within her form. She is the meaning of your devotional songs.'

The next song says:

> 'The goddess of Creation,
> Again
> Descending on the world of life,
> Gave her command
> To Rāmini:
> The essence of prayer
> Is the passionate love,
> Freed from the hold of possessiveness.
> Transplant your soul in Chandidās
> To reach the heaven,
> The changeless land.
> Let loving and prayer
> Unite in joy:
> In Rādhā and Krishna
> And their eternal love.
> Any digression is adultery
> Which leads to hell.
>
> Brace your mind
> With unflagging passion,
> Forever marching
> The *Sahaja* way.'

Having established their relationship under the divine inspiration, the two lovers are then led to face the problems imposed by a small village community. The great emphasis placed on Rāmi being a washer-maid, shows how desperately important the break from the accepted norm must have been.

> 'I have taken refuge
> At your feet,
> My only anodyne,

[1] *Vasu:* literally the earth, implying the emotional body. It also represents female energy.

> Rāmi,
> Rādhā is transfigured
> Into your style,
> Freeing love
> From all traces of lust.
> My heart has no repose
> When I do not see you.
>
> My woman,
> My washer-woman,
> You are the light of my eyes,
> Close as my necklace of flowers.
> You are as a parent to me,
> Junction of the umbilical tie.
> You are the meaning of my prayer,
> The goddess of all the gods.
> You are the heaven and the earth,
> My very universe.
> All is darkness but you...'

In spite of Chandidās thus declaring that Rāmi was his entire universe, the village society refused to accept the relationship as a divine arrangement.

The Brāhmanas appealed to Chandidās: 'You are bringing confusion to all social norms and religious rites'. His brother Nakul cried, 'We are being treated as fallen ones because of your love. I know that love is outside all religious laws and that a lover, independent of the god, reaches Braja,[1] the land of Krishna. I will invite our kinsmen to a great feast to return you to our fold.'

Chandidās sighed with relief; with tears in his eyes he said, 'Only together with the washer-maid can I return:

> I am dependent on love
> As my only relative,
> Love is my destiny.
> The taste of love
> Enriching me with untold wealth,

---

[1] *Braja* represents the region of North India that includes Mathura, Brindavan, Gokul, Govardhan and the surrounding area where Krishna spent his youth.

> Has raised me to the state
> Of madness. My manners,
> Behaviours, are guided by love
> And in love, you are my brothers.
> For love I can go from door to door,
> Adoring all.'

Chandidās's explanations might have satisfied his brother, Nakul, but obviously the villagers did not yield. Chandidās did not relish Nakul's idea of his making a public testimony of his relationship with Rāmi by offering a feast to the village Brāhmanas for whom he had neither respect nor patience.

Nakul then explains to Chandidās that he himself does not doubt the strength of Chandidās's love for Rāmi and its spiritual value. From these songs it appears that Nakul had great understanding and respect for his difficult brother for whom he also felt a spiritual kinship. But, being more worldly wise, he was better equipped to handle the villagers than Chandidās who, in many ways, was a radical. Gently but firmly Nakul continued to impress upon Chandidās the necessity of preparing a feast for the villagers at which he may clarify the situation. In fact it seems that Nakul, in his anxiety for his brother's welfare, wanted to have the whole affair debated with the villagers and to have Rāmi socially accepted. Otherwise there was no reason why he should have risked offending Chandidās by even suggesting the feast. Chandidās replies:

> 'Nakul, my brother,
> you may decide
> about feasting the kinsmen
> since you wish it.
> My heart
> wholly in love,
> loves all the time—
> eating or sleeping.
> Love rules my mind
> leaving nothing as my own.
> But, Wise One,
> none can say
> that love is small
> even when given
> to a washer-maid.'

Though there was no question of surrendering Rāmi to satisfy outraged society, Chandidās finally accepts this disagreeable plan:

> '...You did not know
> When I achieved love,
> The root of all that exists.
> Love is the nature,
> The riches of the arts,
> Love is the air we breathe.
> Love is our kin
> By birth
> And by marriage,
> How can I deny your wish?...'

Nakul was greatly moved by these words. Throughout, he was convinced that the nature of Chandidās's love was impeccable and therefore the villagers would submit. He told his brother that he would go to every door in the village to invite all to the feast and, if necessary, he would bow with utmost humility to each and every person and listen to anything that they might have to say.

But Rāmi was not happy about all the arrangements being made for the feast and, like Rādhā in Chandidās's songs, she is direct in expressing herself:

> '...I hear
> you have discarded love
> for a feast of relatives.
> People respect you
> and I thought you were wise,
> O Nakul,
> how can you be so mad
> as to bother about castes—
> the lowest sort of love.
> Give up your caste
> for love and the lovers,
> or else, how can you live in India?
> Saying this
> the washer-maid
> left for her home.
> There were tears in her eyes
> and confusion in her heart...'

Disturbed and confused Rāmi then goes to Chandidās, wondering how he could ever accept such a proposition which involved some risk to their relationship.

> 'You are doing well,
> my beloved,
> you are doing well
> by removing the cares of our love.
> You had bound me
> with an adorable tie
> when the freshness of love was there
> but now you are removing
> the cares of our love,
> and you are doing well.
> Wash me out if you wish
> like a black spot
> that you once dared taking.
> You come from a respectable home,
> well known in the village,
> but the restless mind
> of a man in you
> carved the marks of love
> on a rock.
> My only regret is that
> I did not find you
> even by offering myself.
> The washer-maid
> took a deep breath
> and burst into sobs.'

Rāmi could do no more. The whole village was now involved in Nakul's effort to bring Chandidās back to his place in society. There is no suggestion anywhere that Chandidās intended to discard Rāmi to regain his social status as a Brāhmana. On the contrary he made it amply clear that on no account had he any intention of giving up Rāmi. But Rāmi was haunted by fear and a feeling of helplessness:

> 'Under the showering
> *bakula* flowers
> the washer-maid sat

and scratched his name on the earth.
Love is a hangman's noose...'

These songs reveal that, as soon as the Brāhmanas settled down to their meal, Rāmi walked in. Her bold act doubtless caused great consternation. It was unthinkable that a low-born washer-maid should enter the eating premises of high-caste Brāhmanas. But no further songs exist to relate what actually happened at the feast. The manuscript, from which these songs were copied, comes to an abrupt end. The pages that followed the description of the feast were eaten by white ants, thus providing further scope for speculations, further elements for the drama of Chandidās's life.

The above translation reveals that these songs have a balladic quality. And, like most ballads, they are charged with the realism of actuality, the plain facts of a social reportage. It is compatible with the usual Indian custom of recording history in an oblique form—through legends and mythology. But the difference between a ballad and a legend is very great. While the reportage of an event becomes firmly locked in the form of a song, bound by its melody and rhythm, there is much more scope for reshaping, and thus distorting, the facts in a popular legend. For example, once the Chandidās story enters the unrestricted realms of legends, it completely loses its documentary character. The following legendary version is an example of this.

Chandidās became Vishnu, the preserving god of the Hindu Triple-Force and Rāmi his female energy, Shakti. When the desperate washer-maid appeared on the sacred ground where the Brāhmanas were dining pandemonium broke out. The terrified girl ran to the poet for protection while his hands were engaged in serving the Brāhmanas with food. But the problem was soon solved as two more arms sprang out instantly from the shoulders of Chandidās, giving him the shape of Vishnu who has four arms. Chandidās was thus able to console his beloved in an embarrassing social situation whilst continuing to serve his guests.

Various legends follow the feast. One relates that Chandidās was dismissed as the priest of the village temple of the goddess Bāshuli. Pretending to be ill, Chandidās locked himself up in his little hut, refusing to eat or drink. Eventually the village

Brāhmanas came to enquire about Chandidās and found him dead. A series of discussions and arguments ensued and finally the poet's body was carried to the cremation ground. While the Brāhmanas were preparing to set fire to his body, Rāmi, wild with fear of losing her beloved, arrived crying with despair. Like a somnambulist the poet, rising from the pyre, began to dance. Rāmi, overjoyed, joined him in the dance while the Brāhmanas fled fearing that Chandidās had turned into a *Brahmadaitya*, a very powerful and high-caste poltergeist.[1]

Apart from the series of songs bearing the name of the washermaid, Rāmi, as their author, there is little evidence about the last days of Chandidās. It is not known for certain if Rāmi was able to write poetry, or could write at all. Based on these songs by Rāmi, Dinesh Chandra Sen[2] described the poet's end under incredibly tense and violent circumstances:

Requested to sing, Chandidās went to the court of the Nawab of Gaud. The Begum, enchanted by the songs, was very attracted by the poet and confessed these facts boldly to the Nawab. At the Nawab's order Chandidās was tied to the back of an elephant and whipped to death. Rāmi and the Begum together witnessed this cruel execution. Despite his dying agonies, Chandidās's eyes were fixed on Rāmi. While watching, the Begum fainted and never revived. Her death filled Rāmi's heart with respect and she expressed her great grief by touching the feet of the Begum.

These exquisite tragic songs also reveal that Chandidās responded to the attraction of the Begum. Complaining, Rāmi tells him, 'Bāshuli had asked you to love me alone, why did you disregard her command?'

Popular belief about the poet's death insists that he was buried under the roof of the permanent stage in a temple court-yard while singing *kīrtan*—love songs of Rādhā and Krishna. And, according to rumour, the stage was demolished by blasts from the Nawab's guns.[3]

We have no reason to disregard at least the synopsis of the facts as given in the songs and ballads. These simple ballads explain why Chandidās's songs on Rādhā and Krishna are so

---

[1] Quoted in *Vaishnava Mahājan Padāvali*, published by Basumati Sāhitya Mandir, Calcutta. No date.

[2] Quoted in *Chandidās O Vidyāpati*, Shankariprasad Basu, Calcutta, 1960.

[3] *Chandidās O Vidyāpati*, Shankariprasad Basu, Calcutta, 1960.

full of emotional tension. Ultimately these songs, though historically fallible, offer a rounded picture of the poet's life and its possible effect on his work.

BENGALI POETRY

Besides being rich in folk songs and ballads, Birbhum enjoys a unique place in the history of Indian poetry. Jayadeva, who is regarded as the last great poet of the Sanskrit language, came from Birbhum during the twelfth century. Jayadeva's fame, mainly due to a small volume of love songs entitled the *Gīta Govinda*, 'Songs of the Cowherd', spread throughout the country. Even today these Sanskrit songs about the love-making of Rādhā and Krishna are familiar to everyone as far south as the western coasts of Kerala. The impact of the poet Jayadeva penetrated every branch of the arts, including painting and drama, for example the modern *Kathakali* dance-drama.

The history of Jayadeva repeated itself in Rabindranath Tagore, the most celebrated poet of this century whose name was to travel far beyond the frontiers of India. Like Jayadeva, the influence of Rabindranath touched every branch of the arts. He came from the Birbhum district and his fame also began with a small volume of songs, entitled *Gitanjali*.

Between these two literary giants of very different centuries from Birbhum, Chandidās enjoys the distinction of being the father of Bengali poetry. Although numerous major poets were immensely influenced by Jayadeva's *Gīta Govinda*, particularly by its literary technique, it left Chandidās completely untouched. Chandidās was involved with the uncharted realms of the heart and the mind. He was either unaware of, or not interested in the sophisticated world of words with the ornamental and flowery expressions which delighted the connoisseurs of poetry in those days. He wrote in Bengali instead of Sanskrit which was still the language of the educated. He wrote about the most complex emotional experiences in a language understandable to the most uncomplicated and simple peasants.

Chandidās and Jayadeva, however, had one thing in common. Both appear to be great individualists and, in a way, social rebels. Departing from Indian custom, neither were attached to a ruling king as a court poet. They wrote for themselves. Defying the usual convention Jayadeva adapted popular metres to use with his exquisite choice of Sanskrit words. It was literary heresy. Sanskrit had the distinction of being the *Devabhāshā*, the language of the gods, and the metres Jayadeva introduced in the *Gīta Govinda* often came from the profane language of the common people. The result was astounding. Through this bold experiment he brought the vigour of popular rhythms to the sophisticated and linguistic refinement to the uneducated. His treatment of Krishna is also unique. Having first established the divine character of Krishna through the following hymn entitled *Dashāvatāra-stotra*, a hymn to the Ten Re-incarnations, he plunges straight into the drama of erotic love.

The hymn describes the process and the cycle of evolution, stage by stage, through the Ten Re-incarnations of Vishnu, the preserving god of the Hindu Triple-Force:[1]

i

'In the deluge of dissolution
to retain the eternal Vedas,[2]
you who appear in the form of a fish
—like a grand navigator—
glory be to you, O lord of the worlds.

ii

To make the earth lay still
on your tremendous back,
you who adopt the body of a tortoise
and suffer deep scars,
glory be to you, O lord of the worlds.

iii

And then, borne in the body of a boar
you who balance the earth on the tip of your tusk
and the earth emerges
as the shining flaw of the moon,
glory be to you, O lord of the worlds.

---

[1] See Rādhā and Krishna, pp. 38–40.

[2] The Vedas represent the earliest available sacred texts of India. Four in number, they are *Rigveda*, *Yajurveda*, *Sāmaveda* and *Atharvaveda*. While the first three are available in their entirety, *Atharvaveda* exists only in fragments and quotations. The assessed dates about the Vedas vary widely, from 3000 BC to 1500 BC.

iv
You who emerge from the body of a lion-man
of lotus hands with fierce nails
and gore Hiranyakashipu
(who brings evil to the earth),
glory be to you, O lord of the worlds.

v
You who descend on the earth
in the body of the Dwarf
to baffle Bali, the great demon king,
and measure the universe in three long steps,
glory be to you, O lord of the worlds.

vi
Housed in the body of the great Bhrigu,
you who wash the sin-stained earth
with the blood of the Kshatriyas
(the ruling, martial caste),
glory be to you, O lord of the worlds.

vii
As if in a rite for the god of the Space,
you who as Rāma offer precious gifts
—the ten slain heads of Rāvana, the king of the giants—
to the ten directions of the battle field,
glory be to you, O lord of the worlds.

viii
In the body of Haladhara who carries a plough,
your fair skin is draped by the cloud-coloured cloth.
It shrinks on your limbs for fear of your ploughing
and glows like the Jamunā, the blue river,
glory be to you, O lord of the worlds.

ix
You who appear in the body of the Buddha,
O, tender-hearted One,
watching animals killed
you who defy the Vedic sacrificial rites,
glory be to you, O lord of the worlds.

x
To destroy the head-long rush of the *Mlechchhas*[1]
with a fierce
comet-like sword in hand,
you who appear in the body of Kalki,
glory be to you, O lord of the worlds.'

Having accomplished the formality of establishing Krishna as the god, Jayadeva embarks on a different course. Poetry and music, the forest and the river, the cloud and the lightning, the moon and the lotus bloom are all included in a rapture of love-making between Rādhā and Krishna. There is absolutely no separation of one thing from the other. It is an intense poetic union:

'The southern breeze
Is softened by the enchanting
Clove-flavoured vines
And the woodland hut is tuned
By the song of the humming bees
Blended with the cooing of the *kokilas*.[2]
Painful for the parted,
While in this delicious Spring
Krishna dances with the youthful girls.'

The song is set to the springtime mode *Vasanta* Raga, as each song in the *Gīta Govinda* was set to a specific musical mode, such as *Gurjari*, *Vasanta*, *Mālava Gauda* and so on, of the Indian Raga system. This became a convention as it was followed by the later Vaishnava poets in Bengal and elsewhere. For instance, the sixteenth-century poetess Mīrābāi of Rajasthan, who also wrote many beautiful love songs on Krishna, set the following words of her song to the rainy season mode, Raga *Megha Malhāra*:

'Clouds of the month of *shrāvana*,[3]
The longing of *shrāvana*:
Shrāvana enchants my heart

---

[1] *Mlechchhas* represent the white-skinned tribes from the northern countries far beyond the borders of India. These days this term is used for Christians.
[2] *Kokila*, the Indian cuckoo. Its cry is said to represent the perfect fifth of the Indian octave. The bird is associated with spring-time and love.
[3] *Shrāvana:* The monsoon month between the middle of July and the middle of August.

With the sounds of Krishna's steps.
Lightning flash. As the storms rage,
Layer upon layer of gathering clouds
Burst in gentle showers...'

While Jayadeva can be safely described as the last great poet of the Sanskrit language, Vidyāpati (who is said to have been twenty years younger[1] yet a contemporary of Chandidās) and Chandidās can be described as the first great poets of the modern languages of North-east India. Unlike the *Gīta Govinda*, in which the songs are written in a dramatic sequence and from the viewpoint of Krishna, a compulsive lover of feminine charms, the songs of Vidyāpati, each one complete in itself, often give voice to Rādhā:

To all my sadness, friend,
There is no end.
From his flute, a breath of poison
Clouded by limbs,
Forcing its way
Into my ears,
Melting my pride, my heart...'[2]

Her life is completely subordinate to her love for Krishna and her fears and worries are reflected in many of the songs by Vidyāpati:

'Has then my lover been suborned by others?
Has he succumbed to yet another girl
Who also knows the ways of love?...'[3]

Unlike Chandidās, Vidyāpati was greatly influenced by Jayadeva in his choice of words, selection of poetic images and, above all, the description of a purely physical situation such as:

'The season of honey
Enters sweet Brindāvan.
The bees drunk wild

---

[1] 'The Date of Vidyāpati', *Indian Historical Quarterly*, pp. 211–216, 1944, quoted in *Bānglār Bāul O Bāul Gān*, Upendranath Bhattacharya, Calcutta, 1957.
[2] *Love Songs of Vidyāpati*, translated by Deben Bhattacharya, edited by W. G. Archer, London, 1963.   [3] *Ibid.*

With sweet blossom's honey
Float row upon row.
Sweeter still are the lord of love
And the sporting honey-girls.
Sweetness and delight
Blend with the flavour of art.
Instruments ring.
Sweet cymbals crash
As the honey-girls move
With their partners in the dance.
Honeyed steps follow
The songs of sweet delight.'[1]

Chandidās never achieved the descriptive powers of Jayadeva or Vidyāpati. He seldom managed to describe feminine beauty or nature in springtime with the flourish of Vidyāpati or the refinement of Jayadeva. He surpassed these two great poets only when it came to expressing the intensity of feelings. He had neither Jayadeva's masculine robustness nor Vidyāpati's insight into a woman's nature. Yet he was incomparably strong when it came to describing the most fundamental human experience. Although his expressions were mostly related to Rādhā, they could also be attributed to the man, Krishna. Above all, he conveyed his ideas in a few simple words:

'Never have I seen such love,
Nor heard.
Even a blink's delay contains eternity...'

Without any poetic duplicity, but by a simple statement of fact, Chandidās reveals the very soul of Rādhā—her fear of losing Krishna. The infinitesimal moment of blindness during an eyelid's blink is too great a time for Rādhā to endure without seeing Krishna. The whole intensity of Rādhā's feeling is transmitted by the shock of a simple phrase.

Chandidās's Rādhā is direct and sharp:

'I throw ashes at all laws
Made by man or god...
What is the worth

[1] *Love Songs of Vidyāpati*, translated by Deben Bhattacharya, edited by W. G. Archer, London, 1963.

4. NARASIMHA GORING HIRANYAKASHIPU (29)

5. VĀMANA QUELLING BALI (29)

6. VISHNU IN THE BODY OF THE BUDDHA (29)

7. HOLI, THE RITE OF SPRING (82)

> Of your vile laws
> That failed me
> In love?...

Rādhā is not at all the long-suffering woman as depicted by Vidyāpati or Jayadeva. Chandidās's Rādhā comes from a Birbhum village; she does not care for poetic romanticism. Although she cries when hurt, she is of sufficient flesh and blood to retort:

> 'This is love:
> My summit of joy
> And you have hindered...
> Die then,
> You sinful woman,
> Go, die...'

The theme of Rādhā and Krishna's love gave new life and inspiration to the various languages in Indian poetry—Kabir and Surdās in Hindi, Sant Tukārām in Marathi, Mīrābāi in Rajasthani and so on. With Bengali poets this theme, mainly because of Chandidās, provided a much greater and deeper impetus which evolved a new school of poetry known as Vaishnava. Perhaps the reason for the popularity of this theme with the poets was because it satisfied a natural desire for blending facts and fantasy, giving a visual and personal form to an abstract idea of the lover Krishna.

The sixteenth-century Bengali poet Govindadās, who is a master in handling the moods of the traditional Indian drama, expresses in the following poem his mixed feelings of joy in Krishna's return and disgust at his affair with Kubjā, the hunch-back girl from Mathura:

> 'So long in the boundless sky the light of snow...
> Unending scintillation of snow-rays...
>   Lightning frozen in the clouds.
>
> Elaborate, graceful, as the yak-tail plume
> Flourished before the image of God,
>   Loveliness enters the town.

So, Murderer, you raise your bow again.
Lost in your heart, Mādhava,[1] I understand,
Sundered from one, you met many desires,
    Rāi[2] was left alone.

You have held laughing even in the day the
People of moon-flowers, tinctured by a light
    Like a new colour of the sun.

Blossoming like the light of clustered pearls.
Gentle with power the gait of the elephant.
O peerless lover, which of the city-girls
    Met you in love, I'll never know.

Everyone else knows, Govindadās retorts:
Kubjā, the hunchback, now is the new queen.'[3]

    The divine lovers are led, stage by stage, through every emotional experience that is the lot of mortal lovers. It is only in the final union of Rādhā and Krishna that their divine characters are completely revealed. Both disappear in one another becoming simply two names. They are called lightning and cloud, not merely as metaphors but as the basic forces of the universe struggling to meet one another. Both the elements, love and violence, are moving side by side like two rivers eager to meet in the sea of life. The lovers of heaven and the forces of the earth are made to meet in a physical union as described by the poet Jnānadās:

> 'Given over, both, to the combat of delight—
> Unflagging lightning in new clouds of rain:
> Rādhā and Kāna[4] on a couch of flowers.
> Both hearts inveigled by the mind-born god,
> Again and again they kiss with startled eyes,
> Her little breasts ravished by violent nails.
> To see them at their love-play in the bower,
> What joy reigns in the heart of Jnānadās.'[5]

[1] Mādhava: Krishna.   [2] Rāi: Rādhā
[3] This poem was translated by Deben Bhattacharya in collaboration with the late Lewis Thompson.   [4] Kāna: Krishna.
[5] This poem was translated by Deben Bhattacharya in collaboration with the late Lewis Thompson.

Modern Bengali poets, on the other hand, did not concern themselves with the convention of the Vaishnava symbolism although the impact of Chandidās can be found in the bare directness of their poetic expression. Understandably the Krishna of the Vaishnava age has today become an abstract character. For the modern Bengali poet he is of little interest as the gay, dark god who carried a flute to entice the cow-girls. Krishna has shed all his old appearance and ornaments yet without losing his powers. Here he is, still vigorous, but only as darkness and sound:

>'Wipe out the sky today,
>Paint the night dark,
>Drown the moon
>In thick mascara of sleeplessness.
>Cover my eyes with your silent feet,
>Come through the bulwark of wind,
>Through the muffled sound of the sea,
>Holding your breath,
>Come, quickly.
>Naked, let us meet
>In the stillness of dark,
>In the empty space of sleepless night,
>Face to face.
>Break the earth into pieces,
>Spread it in the sky,
>With darkness, come in me.'[1]

The images remain. The darkness and the moon. But today they are used as contrasts not as complements to one another. In the next poem it is obvious that the symbolism used by a modern Bengali poet differs utterly from the Vaishnava symbolism of the bees and the lotus, or the cloud and the lightning. Through the symbolism of quick-sand in contrast with that of the horseman, the poet Bishnu Day has simply shifted from the mediaeval images to more tense, modern ones but not entirely removed in spirit from the directness of Chandidās. This change of emphasis, however, has produced an interesting situation. Unlike the lightning illuminating the

[1] Translated excerpt from *Abhipsā*, 'Wish', by Bishnu Day, born 1909.

dark sombre clouds, the image of the modern beloved, the quick-sand, while begging him for action, is desperately eager to devour her 'horseman':

> 'Tidal waves on human sea,
> My heart, a sandy island.
> Quick-sand, I call far away,
> Where are you, Horseman?...
> Rise and fall call in your eyes...
> Where is your action?
>
> Love, my beloved,
> Desire simmers in space,
> Will you not offer your promise
> Upon my body?...
>
> Raise your spear with a light air,
> Beyond the rivers and the seven seas—
> Fill your heart with a light air
> And ruthlessly crush my timid doors.
> Here, the hills with a light air
> Weave dreams of storms and hail and snow.
>
> My desire in the shape of a shadow
> Follows your steps,
> Pressed to your body.
> My breath, my body, trembles with desire,
> My desire halts a glacier...'[1]

The experiences of daily problems were not unfamiliar to the era of the Vaishnava poems. But these were simply not regarded as suitable matter for poetry. In contrast, today in Bengal, social and political consciousness has supplemented—in many cases almost replaced—the religious awareness of the Vaishnava epoch. Inquiry into God is now seldom undergone with the lyrical subjectivity and submission that is found in the Vaishnava poems; this, also, is now involved with 'social consciousness':

[1] Translated excerpt from *Ghodsawār*, 'Horseman' by Bishnu Day, born 1909.

> 'He will merge the stormy wind
> With the broken doors
> Of that crumbling house,
> He will merge.
> You wouldn't shudder at the wild gust!
> In famine, in fire,
> Stray dogs, thirsty, we lick the fields
> Flooded, in pouring rain.
> The earth is floating on its final tears.
> He will merge them all...'[1]

This transfer of attitude has produced an acute awareness of self-preservation—preservation of the individual in a modern, mass society. In one of his poems the poet Samar Sen examines the city life of Calcutta and realizes the boredom involved:

> 'Our sleep ends
> As the distorted day dawns from the night's
> Poisoned blood
> And the sky grows heavy,
> Tuned in our boring work,
> Exhaustion,
> The hooter blows.
> Beyond us roar the fast buses...'[2]

With his faith challenged by insecurity, the modern poet is caught by a primitive desire for self-preservation which he conveys with a brutal directness that can also be found in many of Chandidās's poems. Samar Sen continues:

> '...Brahma, Jesus, Rāmakrishna,
> In time I trust them all;
> Yet, in dangerous days, unnaming worries,
> In my unsteady wits
> I trust only the straight simple words:
> Nothing so lasting as a heavy purse...'

Thus, the poet simply follows a tradition in Bengali poetry established by Chandidās, a social rebel of his time. Samar Sen

[1] Translated excerpt from *Sangati*, 'Unity', by Amiya Chakrabarty, born 1901.
[2] Translated excerpt from *Nāgarik*, 'The Citizen' by Samar Sen, born 1916.

ends his poem by parodying the well-known lines of a *Sahaja* poem by Chandidās, touching the very essence of the modern spirit:

> 'I am the greatest truth of all,
> Nothing beyond.'[1]

RĀDHĀ AND KRISHNA

Creation, preservation and dissolution are regarded by the Hindus as the three basic factors of life and these are attributed to the *Trishakti*, the Triple-Forces—Brahmā, Vishnu and Shiva. Vaishnava philosophy is based on Vishnu, the Preserver. The term Vaishnava is derived from the same root as Vishnu. Krishna, who figures as the hero of the Vaishnava poems, is a reincarnation of Vishnu and Rādhā, his female counterpart. The followers of this faith are known as Vaishnavas.

In these poems, signed by Chandidās, Dwija Chandidās and Badu Chandidās, both Rādhā and Krishna are introduced by several other names. Rādhā, for example, is often addressed by her colloquial Bengali name Rāi. It expresses certain affection, a particular warmth of familiarity. Similarly, Krishna is often called Shyām, Kālā, Kāliyā, Kānu and so on, depending on the mood of the poem. For instance, while the name Kānu conveys certain endearing qualities in the character of Krishna, Kālā expresses the disturbing elements of his nature. These different names for Rādhā and Krishna also greatly helped the poets to avoid repetition.

The earliest description of Krishna's life[2] is available through a brief reference to Krishna as a student of philosophy. It is mentioned in the *Chhāndogya Upanishad* which, in its present form, is considered to have been written during the sixth century BC. At this time the character of Krishna emerges as a hero and a leader in the *Mahābhārata*, the great Indian epic which was compiled during several centuries, possibly starting from about the fourth century BC. In the *Bhagavad-Gītā*, which is fairly well known to English readers, Krishna appears as a teacher

---

[1] Translated excerpt from '*For Thine is the Kingdom*' by Samar Sen, born 1916. It is interesting to note that though the poem is written in Bengali, the title of the poem, as written above, is in English.

[2] For a detailed study of Krishna's character, see *The Loves of Krishna*, W. G. Archer, London, 1957.

and a guide to Arjuna during the Mahābhārata war, and it is here we find Krishna revealing his divine character in the most precise terms: 'Renouncing all the ways of religions, take shelter in Me alone.' This statement is an important factor in the development and growth of the Vaishnava faith and the *Sahaja* movement within its fold.

The most complete account of Krishna's life is available in a monumental work entitled the *Bhāgavata Purāna* from the ninth or tenth century. It leads us, by various stages, from Krishna's childhood to Krishna as a young cowherd and describes his encounters with various demons, his conquests of evil forces to protect the community, his adventures with the cowgirls, his marriage with Rukmini and finally the scene of his death at the hand of a hunter while he was resting under a fig tree.

It is in the *Bhāgavata Purāna* that we first meet Rādhā who was later to become the very soul of the Vaishnava poems. She is introduced as a married girl and the daughter of a cowherd named Vrishabhānu. Her husband Āyāna was a brother of Yashodā, Krishna's foster mother in Gokula. The appearance of Rādhā and her love for Krishna unlocked a tidal wave. It flooded the whole of India, the north and the south, incessantly for over five hundred years, blending divine love with sensual fervour, religiousness with poetry, music and painting.

In the field of Vaishnava theology and spiritual leadership, great teachers like Rāmānujāchārya (AD 1037–1137), followed by Mādhvācharya (AD 1199–1303), Nimbārka and Vallabhācharya (born 1479) and finally Shri Chaitanya (AD 1486–1533) born in Nabadwip in West Bengal, were undoubtedly the five most important Vaishnava leaders who headed the movement in their times and who still have a large following all over India. It was Shri Chaitanya who particularly influenced the Bengali Vaishnava poets in the period which followed him.

According to the philosophy of Shri Chaitanya, the god is indivisible. There could be no division between the creator and the created. He is beyond the limits of human thought, that is why this ephemeral world appears neither divided nor undivided from Him. Krishna, therefore, with all his apparently worldly attributes, is neither an image nor a reincarnation. He is the God.

The Vaishnava approach to the god is through two of His

attributes: *aishvarya* and *mādhurya*. *Aishvarya* represents the majestic quality, the inconceivable, the immensity of His all-pervading power. The devotee must concentrate on the greatness of the god. The devotee of the *mādhurya* aspect utilizes the compulsive power of his own emotions in trying to find union with the god. He loves the god with a fervour equalling those of Rādhā's intense passion, of Yashodā's obsessive maternal affection for her foster son Krishna, and of Sudāmā's devoted friendship for Krishna the cowherd. Since all his feelings are already attributed to the god, how can a devotee abandon any one of them? The path of devotion or *bhakti* is the merger of all these emotions and feelings.[1]

Chaitanya believed in the path of *bhakti*: the love for Krishna must be for Krishna alone, neither distracted by His great powers nor by any spiritual ambitions such as *nirvāna* or *moksha* (the freedom from rebirth, from the repetitive cycle of life and death). It must be like the love of a lover who is free from any motive other than the very act of loving.

THE SONGS

The mood of Chandidās's love songs about Rādhā and Krishna reflects the spirit of *bhakti*.[2] He wrote these songs for a listening audience rather than a reading public. The impact was immediate and the audience increased steadily. These love songs of Rādhā and Krishna have been acclaimed by the public, like popular entertainments, for nearly five hundred years.

Great traditions of professional *Kīrtan*—songs-of-praise singers—have developed around the songs by Chandidās and other poets who wrote on the theme of Rādhā and Krishna's romance. Even today, it is not necessary to look very far to find a *Kīrtan* singer, accompanied by a chorus, a pair of *khol* drums and cymbals, addressing his audience in an open-air temple courtyard or on a village green with these songs, which he then elaborates and explains by an extempore commentary in half chant. Since a performance of *Kīrtan* often lasts for several hours, the technique of presentation is an important factor. Each legend of the Krishna episode is treated as a compact unit, a *pālā*. Sometimes the entire Krishna legend is serialized

---

[1] These feelings are classified as peace (*shānta*), servitude (*dāsya*), affection for the child Krishna (*vātsalya*), friendship (*sakhya*), and the finer qualities of erotic love (*mādhurya*).   [2] See Rādhā and Krishna, pp. 38–40.

over a period of weeks but broken into different *pālās*, with each *pālā* offering a sequence to the main episode.

The success of a *pālā kīrtan* depends upon the standard of the commentary on the songs. Sometimes the songs and the spoken words are alternated by an instrumental interlude on the *khol* drum and the cymbals. Since the audience is too familiar with the story to tolerate monotony, the presentation must be original.

The sequence of Mathura, or the *Māthur pālā*, for instance, is a very popular theme among the *kīrtan* singers. Krishna is presented in this as a free spirit. He wanders, even when he is surrounded by love with all its binding force; he must leave Brindāvan, the place where his devoted friends and the cowgirls and his beloved Rādhā yearn for him. But he must go to save his kinsmen and the city of Mathura from its demon king Kamsa. When Kamsa is duly slain, Krishna does not return to Brindāvan. Gossip about a hunch-back girl and her devotion to a responsive Krishna reaches Brindāvan and a friend of Rādhā goes to seek Krishna in the rich city of Mathura.

> 'It is a disgrace,
> Krishna,
> Such evil thoughts took hold of you.
> I did not entreat you to make love
> While you in your heart
> Toyed with strange designs.
> You have never known the sense of shame,
> Beloved friend,
> Nor any trace of love.
> While this land
> Still twists in flames,
> You are out to set fire to another land...
>
> Says Chandidās
> With a heart torn by pain:
> The golden goddess
> Rolls in the dust,
> And Kubjā the hunch-back,
> Shares Krishna's bed.'[1]

[1] Quoted in *Vaishnava Padalahari*, edited by Durgadas Lahiri, Calcutta, 1905, and also tape-recorded by Deben Bhattacharya in Birbhum. It was sung by one of the members of the Mitra-Thakur family, the well-known *kīrtan* singers of Mayanadal, Birbhum.

Shri Chaitanya is credited with being the father of modern *kīrtan* singing, accompanied by drums and cymbals.

The music of the *kīrtan* suggests a popular trend. This displays a strong tendency towards blending styles and types. One of the oldest styles of classical Indian singing, the *dhrupad*, is often interwoven with popular folk melodies and styles. The most favoured rhythm of the *kīrtan* singers is the *gad khemtā* which is also related to a popular type of dance. The *khemtā* dance of the dancing girls was one of the chief entertainments of feudal Bengal, but we have no information whether the *kīrtan* singers adopted this rhythm from the *khemtā* dancers, or the reverse.

The rhythm *gad khemtā* uses twelve beats, divided into two bars of six each: one bar gives the base sound and the other the treble, alternately. The accent on the beat is introduced when the tempo changes, or when the mood of the song varies.

For instance, in the song from the *Māthur pālā*, quoted above, which expresses sarcasm, the drummers accentuate the first and the fourth beats of each bar. The following song, however, in conveying a simple expression of sorrow, adopts unaccentuated beats until the tempo changes. This, too, is from the *Māthur pālā* and is signed by Dwija Chandidās.

> 'Rāi[1] laid the snare with her eyes
> And caught the beautiful parrot
> Shyām[2]
> She held him, adoring,
> In the cage of her ribs,
> Tying him by the chain of her heart.
> Taming him,
> She tended him
> And fed him on the nectar of her love.
> She taught him how to speak:
> Rādhā, Rādhā, Rādhā.
>
> But the faithless bird
> Cut the link of her chain
> To fly away to Mathura,
> And Kubjā the hunch-back
> Held him there.'[3]

[1] Rādhā. [2] Krishna.
[3] Quoted in *Vaishnava Padalahari*, edited by Durgadas Lahiri, Calcutta, 1905, this song was also tape-recorded by Deben Bhattacharya while the

Judged by average standards, Krishna's behaviour may appear heartless but the heart plays no role in this tale. Literary licence may permit him to be presented as a character, but he is not treated as one. He represents the very act of loving: always alive to the vibrations of love, to the perennial presence of an

distinguished *kīrtan* singer, Shri Tarapada Kundu, sang it to a large audience in the Coochbehar Kali Temple of Benares. The song is written in the metre entitled *Dīrgha-Tripadī*.

The poet Jayadeva also frequently uses this metre in his *Gīta-Govinda*. In Sanskrit, with its clear-cut pronunciation, it is easy to utilize the time measure in a more organized fashion. The short vowel is treated as one time unit and the long vowel and the double consonant as two time units. In Sanskrit, the time-division of the *Dīrgha-Tripadī* is a precise 8+8+8+4 or 3, such as

```
chandanacharchitanīlakalevarapītavasanabanamālī
└──────┘└──────┘└──────┘└──┘
   8        8        8      4
kelichalanmanikundalamanditagandayugasmitashālī
└──────┘└──────┘└──────┘└──┘
   8        8        8      4
```

The most favoured metre in the works of Chandidās is also the *Dīrgha-Tripadī*, but, having no use for the Sanskrit pronunciation, Chandidās's *Dīrgha Tripadī* assumed the character of the Bengali language. It is free from the accents of the long vowels and the double consonants.

Depending on the mood that a reader or a singer wishes to emphasize, he can add his intonation on a given word. So a short vowel can be extended into a long one or a long vowel reduced to a short one. Therefore, in Bengali *Dīrgha Tripadī* the number of syllables is considered of greater importance than the precise time units of the Sanskrit metre. For instance, in this particular case, Chandidās employs twenty syllables to a line, divided by 6+6+8. The line is broken in three sections following the division of the syllables:

        Shyāma shuka pākhi   sundara nirakhi
           (Rāi) dharila nayana phānde
        Hridaya pinjare   rākhila sādare
           manohi shikale bāndhe

The basic melody of the song is transcribed below:

impermanent force. Everyone, from the prettiest girl to the ugliest hunch-back, has drawn upon his ever-flowing stream of love. Even when Krishna appears to be calmly settled in Mathura, we find him reacting to the memory of Brindāvan as intensely as any mortal lover. He says:

'I could not suffer the least delay for fear of missing you. I could not live without you. I could not think of our bodies parted for even a moment. When in delight the hair of our bodies rose, it seemed like a mountain wall between us. Day and night, we lived that way.

'How can I live now?

'Rādhā is far away and I in Mathura. And life continues. A lovely city, the new city-girls and so much wealth around, yet all are useless without Rādhā. My eyes fill with tears. In my startled heart, I hear the girls of Brindāvan and the ripples of the river Jamunā.'[1]

Though Krishna is presented as a great and contradictory enigma, his character emerges through the supreme achievements of the Indian arts—painting, music and poetry. The poets do not treat him with the reverence due to the god; they treat him with the equality of a fellow being, but attributing qualities —both good and bad—on a supernatural scale. They taunt him, they laugh at him, they get angry with him, but ultimately he emerges as a character who is eternally lovable.

THE SAHAJA MOVEMENT

Sahaja means that which is inborn, spontaneous. The poems on the theme of Sahaja were never written for literary reasons. These were strictly meant for a private group of initiates into the Sahaja faith:

> 'Listen O, brother man,
> Man is the greatest Truth
> Of all,
> Nothing beyond.'

These lines from a poem bearing the name of Chandidās as its author came as a great surprise to the modern intellectuals of

[1] *Love Songs of Vidyāpati*, translated by Deben Bhattacharya, edited by W. G. Archer, London, 1963.

Bengal. They appeared with the vitality of a new discovery—a discovery of the truth in man written in the most simple and direct terms. They had the freshness of a new idiom in comparison with the vast complexities of Sanskrit religious literature where gods and demons abound and, by and large, the medium of allegory flourishes with the rich flavour of ornamental words. Since their debut in Bengali literature, these lines have become as common as a popular proverb.

The foundation of the Sahaja movement is involved with the Hindu method of *yoga*. Yoga means 'union' and is a disciplinary defence against losing track of oneself. The process involves strict self-discipline, including control of the body and mind. Different exercises are prescribed for controlling the functions of one's body, the process of feeling and the mechanism of thought. *Yoga* represents the union of the matter and the spirit. Consciousness is its main vehicle, and the path of *yoga* is a cautious one which abstains from taking risks.

By contrast the Sahaja path runs in a bold direct line. Unlike *Yoga* it uses tension as a means for imparting consciousness. Instead of suppressing what is regarded to be weakness, it exploits it so as to be free from it. Great emphasis is laid on an antipathy for the desire to possess. Possessiveness is another name for pollution and, as the poet says,

> 'Pollution tends to make
> Its rendezvous in hell.'

To a Sahaja follower, his body is as sacred as Krishna himself and his love equally so:

> 'Using one's body
> As a medium of prayer
> And loving spontaneously
> Is the Sahaja love.'

If the god has given us the body, he is inevitably involved with it, with every fibre of our limbs:

> 'God is the only way.
> If god leaves
> Strength leaves.
> If god goes
> Body goes.'

In spite of such preoccupation with the 'man' and his 'body' as vehicles of spirituality, the Sahaja poets draw a line when it comes to lust. Even though violent passion and erotic love are highly praised, mere sensuality without any deeper feeling behind it is condemned outright:

> 'A man can march
> To his funeral, in lust.
> But a lover drinks the nectar
> Sieving poison out.'

The stage of being in love is the stage of being aware of existence itself. It is a state of alertness to each vibration of life:

> 'A connoisseur
> Draws out love
> With tender care
> From the pulsation of leaves,
> From the rays of the flower.'

The conventions of Hindu society never accepted the Sahaja path because of its erotic nature. The Sahaja faith blandly preached erotic love as the easiest and quickest means to that self-realization which is the ultimate aim of the Hindu religious belief. Basically the Hindu religion is extremely democratic—in spite of the caste system, which developed like vast trade unions with a rigidity equal to that of the trade unions of modern times—and it had no power to suppress the Sahaja movement. What disturbed the Hindu society most was the Sahaja claim that an erotic relationship of spiritual nature can only take place with a woman who belongs to another man. Love-making is one of the important aspects of the Sahaja worship since every man is Krishna and every woman is Rādhā, and the contact between the two is their devotion, their intense awareness of one another:

> 'The essence of beauty
> springs
> from the eternal play
> of man as Krishna
> and woman as Rādhā.

>   Devoted lovers
>   in the act of loving
>   seek to reach
>   the goal.'

This awareness for one another can be made constant, according to the Sahaja interpretation, only if the lovers were not socially contracted to marriage.

It is a physical fact that a lover is far more tense and alert when his deepest love is beyond his immediate reach. In Sahaja love, the lovers must be individuals in their own rights: like a cloud and the lightning, the flute and the fingers. It is only then that they can together produce the sacred love of the Sahaja. And it is only possible when both the lovers are conscious as Chandidās describes it: 'It is like being able to extend your person to the very limit of space—east and west, north and south, all directions having an immediate meaning and all at once.' For an ideal Sahaja lover:

>   'Nothing is far away,
>   Everything is near:
>   The Universe
>   And the painting on the wall.'

The Sahaja movement lasted throughout several centuries. During the period of the Pal kings of Bengal, Buddhism spread at a great speed, and between the ninth and the eleventh centuries it reached the majority of the lowest strata of the society in a very particular form called *Sahajayāna* or the Spontaneous Vehicle. It had its roots in the earlier *Tāntrik* religion of Bengal. In Sahajayāna, the pleasure of the senses were blended with the quests of the spirit. It was a synthesis of the two extremes of luxury and austerity. It grew as a popular rebellion against the high-brow Buddhist conventionalism which emphasized only austerity. The non-intellectual, the working class, which formed the so-called 'lower castes' embraced this religion on a mass scale. But, it was by no means confined solely to the unsophisticated. The Mayanāmati copper plate, dated 1220, describes the Prime Minister of the King Ranabankamalla of Pattikeraka as an adherent of the Sahaja faith.[1]

---

[1] Indian Historical Quarterly, Vol. IX, p. 282.

Pattikeraka is claimed by historians to have been situated where today lies the district of Comilla in East Pakistan. This fact also proves that the Sahaja faith had spread throughout Bengal.

Following the Buddhist Pal kings, Bengal was ruled by the Sens who were Vaishnavas.[1] They ruled from the beginning of the twelfth century until the middle of the thirteenth. During this period the poet Jayadeva wrote his *Gīta Govinda* which influenced all India. Under the patronage of the Sen kings the Vaishnava religious movement, adopting the theme of Rādhā and Krishna, began to flourish, and alongside it the Sahaja movement also began to spread, but within a closed circle of initiates. For all practical purposes it was hardly different from the Buddhist Sahajayāna movement. It merely changed its surface identity. The 'cause' became Krishna and the 'effect' Rādhā. Love represented the Spirit and desire Matter. The process of transition from the Buddhist Sahajayāna to the Vaishnava Sahaja movement was exceptionally smooth. From Jayadeva's hymn to the Ten Reincarnations of Vishnu we have already seen that the Buddha, instead of being treated as a rebel, was adopted as the ninth reincarnation of Vishnu, the preserving godhead of the Hindu Triple-Force. It was easy for Jayadeva to give the Buddha this status because Buddha's rebellion was against conventionalism in Hindu society and religion during the fifth century BC.

But when the Muslims overran Bengal during the mid-thirteenth century they introduced a totally alien spirit, a particular type of puritanism that had developed in the austere life of the Arabian desert. The result was systematic destruction. Great monasteries such as Odantapura, the architecture of which was copied in Tibet and described as an 'incomparable, unchangeable holy place arisen through miraculous means',[2] and Vikramshila, were laid in ruins and the Buddhist monks and nuns massacred.[3] This happened during the Bengalis' first encounter with the invaders before the latter settled down to proselytizing, a process which continued for several centuries. The victims were mostly the uneducated and the poor of Hindu

[1] See Rādhā and Krishna, pp. 38–40.
[2] Quoted in *The Religions of Tibet*, Helmut Hoffmann, London, 1961.
[3] *Bānglār Bāul O Bāul Gān*, p. 128, Upendranath Bhattacharya, Calcutta, 1957.

8. RAGA VASANTA (30)

9. RĀSA MANDALA (31)

10. RĀSA LĪLĀ (31)

11. BIRTH OF KRISHNA (39)

society, many of whom belonged to the Sahaja faith. Before the end of the thirteenth century, most of Bengal was under the political domination of the Muslims.

During this period, Islam in the Middle Eastern world—from where it travelled to India—was undergoing certain inherent changes. Sufi mysticism was gaining ground as the Turkish and Persian elements in Islam began to exert themselves. Jalalu'l Dīn Rūmī of Konya, Turkey, who is considered one of the greatest of the thirteenth-century mystics, was writing divine love poems such as this:

> "'Tis the flame of Love that fired me
> 'Tis the wine of Love inspired me.
> Wouldst thou learn how lovers bleed,
> Hearken, hearken to the Reed!'[1]

Finally it was in Sufism that the converts from the Sahaja path found a kindred spirit, and some of the Sufi members among the ruling Muslim population reciprocated the Sahaja understanding of Sufism by embracing the Sahaja ways. The contact was immediate. As a result, a number of Sufi poets became interested in the Sahaja movement and the Sahaja poets studied Sufi doctrines. Though any form of image worship is forbidden in Islam, the Sahaja-Sufis continued using the theme of Rādhā and Krishna's love as part of their faith even though Rādhā and Krishna are often depicted in sculptures and paintings.

While numerous caste Hindus and Buddhists were killed or forced to embrace Islam during the process of proselytization, the Sahaja doctrine maintained its identity by its very nature, the spontaneous way, as it did from the early period before Buddhism adopted it. With the arrival of Islam in Bengal there came into being two types of Sahaja devotees who diverged from the opposing Hindu and Moslem societies. While the Hindu followers of the Sahaja faith remained mainly Krishna worshippers, the Muslims introduced Allah.

Most of the interesting Sahaja poems are attributed to the names of Chandidās, Dwija Chandidās and Badu Chandidās. As in the songs about Rādhā and Krishna, the poetic style is very similar from one song to the next despite the different

[1] *RŪMĪ—Poet and Mystic*, Reynold A. Nicholson, London, 1956.

signatures. A Dīn Chandidās also wrote Sahaja poems, but of extremely poor poetic merit. We have no means of ascertaining whether the great Chandidās, the poet of the most beautiful Rādhā and Krishna songs, composed some of these Sahaja poems or not. The language of the poems of the oral tradition is a dynamic language; it cannot be static, for like the Sahaja movement, it changes from age to age.

In final analysis, it appears that the whole Sahaja movement might have started as a class or caste movement, a rebellion against social conventions. The Buddhists were against the caste system, but in effect they were against *Brāhmanic* intellectual domination. The *Kshatriyas*, or the martial caste, assumed both political power and control of the intelligentsia. Their smashing of the rigid trade unions of the caste system chiefly affected the three upper castes: the *Brāhmanas*, the intellectual and the priestly caste; the *Kshatriyas*, the martial and the ruling caste; and the *Vaishyas*, the merchants. It was mostly the *Shudras*, the working-class castes, who found a great release in the *Sahajayāna*. A *Domni*, a woman belonging to the lowest caste who was literally untouchable, was the most ideal partner for ritualistic love-making that would bring a devotee nearer the ultimate Truth. What could be more revolutionary than this? An untouchable woman was worshipped as the main-spring of spiritual experience.

Obviously, by the time the Vaishnava Sen kings came to power in Bengal, the caste system had relaxed considerably under Buddhist rule. The preachers of the Sahaja movement sought a different code to rebel against. This time, instead of the caste system, it was the convention of marriage. The beloved, who shares the devotee's search for Krishna, must belong socially to another man. The Bengali word for such a woman is *parakīyā*, a woman who is owned by another man. In fact, from available evidence it appears that the soul of the Sahaja movement is tension.

The arrival of Islam in Bengal caused no major change in the Sahaja ways. The members of the faith simply adopted Allah alongside Krishna, while believing neither in Islamic nor in Hindu religious conventions. The Sahaja movement's heyday in both poetry and religion was in the seventeenth century, during the last phase of Islamic rule in Bengal.

Following Islamic domination the British ruled in Bengal.

During the eighteenth century the Sahaja movement was still strong but then came the Victorian period accompanied by its dull mediocrity. Besides decadent love-making, the *Sahajiyās*[1] contributed little in those days.

Artificial respiration had no place in Sahaja philosophy nor did the *Sahajiyās* have any feeling for politics. As urban society adopted the puritanical tenets of the administrative and mercantile bureaucracy during the Victorian era, the peasants who formed the great majority of the Indian population were pushed back into the villages. There was no coercion involved—rather it was a psychological inevitability resulting from the rule of an alien civilization which introduced a class structure which was superimposed on the existing deeply rooted caste system. The various nuances of the British class structure are still unknown in Indian society, but the stream-lining of the urban and village societies and their rigid separation from one another took place during this period. The *Sahajiyās*, who were accustomed to the caste system of the Hindu tradition, were at a loss. In spite of caste divisions, it was a traditional society. It had a fundamental unity. But, faced with this new dilemma, the *Sahajiyās* found themselves out of date, and out of step. So, since the middle of the nineteenth century, they have been dormant. Even now, a few old men and women are still alive who call themselves the followers of the Sahaja faith, but it is quite apparent that they are waiting for death.

[1] *Sahajiyā* means he who follows the *Sahaja* path.

LOVE SONGS OF CHANDIDĀS

I

The evening dew
  is forming
    on the leaves...

O please,
  go and see,
I can hear him...

2

What sudden sound from the *kadamba* wood,
Startled my ears!
What essence of life,
Sweetness and poetry
Raised sadness and wonder in my heart!
How can I describe
The stir?...
The sound persists from the enticing flute
As poison and life...

3

Who was that girl?
Friend, who was that girl
Inflaming the river
With her fair skin?...

The gold necklace
On the peaks of her breasts
Shone as the moon on the mountain snow.
The darkness in tears,
The shadows of the moon,
A flood of black hair rolled on her hips.
She rose from the river
Like a slice of the moon,
Glistening in twilight dark.
As I stood watching
And loosing myself,
She walked away wringing and twisting my soul
Together with her sari—dripping, blue.
My heart still shivers in a fever of love...

4

What magic did you play, my love,
To confuse my life, my timid heart?
My days are changed into nights
And the nights into days.
My home has become the open space
And the whole space my privacy.
Those who were close are strangers to-day
And those who were strangers are akin to me.
Is that the meaning of your love, my darling?...

5

Like frozen lightning her fair face
I saw at the river bank,
Hair plaited as a coiled snake
Dressed with jasmin lace...
Her darting glance and gentle smile
Made me eager.
Throwing and catching a ball of flowers,
She revealed in full her youthful form.
As her breasts rebelled against her dress,
Her face was bright with mischievous smiles.
And feet adorned with ankle-bells,
Were painted red.

6

Danger grew
That evil day
As I held in my wide open eyes
Krishna.
I saw my life go.
Erupting with the fire of love,
My heart throbbed for nothing else
From that very day.

Water may kill a small fire
But how can I fight the holocaust
Of heart?
A burning forest rouses the world
Through flames,
But the embers of my heart
Ignite unseen...

7

Never have I seen such love,
Nor heard.
Even a blink's delay contains eternity.
Clasped to my breasts you are far from me.
Stay as my veil close to my face,
How I fear when you turn your eyes away!
We spend the night: one body,
Sinking in the fathomless ocean of joy.
As the dawn comes our anxious hearts watch
Life deserting us.

8

I never touch a black flower
In my diffidence.
Sadness grows.
I hear everywhere
Whispers about my dark love.

I never look at the sombre cloud
Fearing Krishna.
I do not wear kohl.
I screen my eyes
While going to the stream.
As I pass by
The *kadamba* shade,
I seal my ears
Hearing the flute.

9

One day
Walking with my sister-in-law,
I thought of beloved Shyām.
Emotions filled my heart
And I stood still.
My body went beyond control
Trembling, trembling.

10

I was pouring some water
That looked black
And I remembered Krishna.
In sleep and in dream
I constantly see
Only my Krishna.

I leave my black hair down,
I never dress it.
And I never wear black mascara in my eyes...

12. KRISHNA AT THE BREAST OF HIS FOSTER MOTHER, JASHODĀ (39)

13. KĀLIYA DAMANA (39 and note 1, p.96)

14. KĀLIYA DAMANA (39 and note 1, p. 96)

15. KRISHNA FERRYING THE COW-GIRLS ACROSS THE RIVER JAMUNĀ (39)

11

Please do not tell me
For which woman's bower
He has abandoned
Me.
Meeting with raptures
In a new-found love,
He has ejected me from his memory.
She must be brilliant
In the arts of ardour,
She must know all about the passion-play.
My lover is inveigled
By her combat of delight...

12

You took so long to return,
Dearest,
I nearly died
And we would never have met.
But a woman can bear
The pain that would break a rock.
My days of sadness
Sadly crawled
And I did not care.
I felt fine since you were glad.

And did the city[1] treat you well,
My sweet?

But all that agony is over, my love,
The jewel that I had lost
Is back to my arms again.

Let then the kokila[2] come and sing
And the bees hum
And the southern breeze may also blow
As the moon ascends the sky.

---

[1] The city of Mathurā, where Krishna went to live as a king with Kubjā, the hunch-back queen.
[2] The Indian cuckoo, the symbol of spring and love.

13

I throw ashes at all laws
Made by man or god.
I am born alone,
With no companion.
What is the worth
Of your vile laws
That failed me
In love,
And left me with a fool,
A dumbskull?[1]

My wretched fate
Is so designed
That he is absent
For whom I long.
I will set fire to this house
And go away.

---

[1] It refers to Āyāna, Rādhā's husband.

14

I harbour in my heart
My lonesome thoughts,
With loving care.

Those who define
The ways of life
Not even knowing
What feeling means,
Double my pain.

He who evades
My seeking eyes
In real life
And in dream
Forever dwells
In me...

15

I will not treat again
My eyes
With the image of delight,
I will seal
My ears
From the name of love.
That fiendish word
Brings untold hazards.
Whether in my dream
Or in my thought,
Never shall I bear
Love's passion-play.
I will disown this city of love
And my life
Of the garden of desire.

I will emigrate
To the depth of the forest,
Away from the virus of love.

16

That terrible love
And my helpless fate.
But I can endure
All.
Friends, look out!
Danger looms
With Krishna's loving.
You will never again be free.

I can leave him
But my love would not go,
And sadness grows...
Sorrow surmounts
My enormous love,
I wish I had loved a little less.
Laughter, laughter
Exploded my loving,
Now tears are my life...

17

I have blackened my golden skin
Longing for him,
Though he was not my husband.
I belonged to a respectable home.
As the fire encircled me,
My life began to wilt.
And my heart,
Brooding eternally,
Parched for my dark darling,
My Krishna...

18

One gnawing pain is my home
And the other is Krishna.
Where else can I go,
O friend,
I have no ways open.
Life sizzling on fire
Singes my limbs,
And words of advice
Pour acid on my heart.
Like the death itself,
Krishna's love
Is beyond remedy...

19

This is love,
My summit of joy
And you have hindered me.
Have you no heart?
Have you no faith?
Die then,
You sinful woman,
Go, die.

I shall not live either
For this sadness...

20

The more I try to restrain them
The more they rebel.

I wish to go a different way
But my feet race along Krishna's path.
My cruel tongue repeats his name
In spite of me.
The more I cover my wretched nose
The more it longs for Shyām's lovely scent.
As I dream of never to hear of him
My ears pursue his name.

Shame on my senses
Which are so absurd,
Shame on their doting
On that black Krishna...

21

Who can understand
The fire, love,
That forever burns?
I bear it as I can.
Who can say
That love is a boon?
Love is disquieting.
My ribs are charred
As I brood and brood.
Tears pour down
And my shameless heart
Is never at rest.
As a second fate,
Love lords my life.

22

What god is that
Who moulded me a woman?
I am always alone
Being married and watched.
Since falling in love
Is a disgrace for me,
I must then kill
My meaningless life.
I am not free
To open my mouth
But I am in rapture
With another man.

23

That son of Nanda
Dropped on my head
A deadly thunderbolt.
And I never even dreamed
That love could be a danger...

24

I took pains in picking the blossoms
To string them in a garland of love.
The coolness of flowers
Faded with the scent,
My neck, I felt, was ablaze.

Why should my gardener do this to me?
He poisoned my garland
Infecting my heart.
With the whole of my person
My heart was set on fire.

I could no longer hear
And I could no longer see.
Flowers were turning into flames..

My heart was singed
And my ribs collapsed,
They sank and sank
And my body wholly dissolved.

25

I can walk the way of love
And let loving be the essence of life.
Nothing is of value
In the ashes of living,
I must swim the lake of love.

The city of desire
Is my domicile,
I leave the rest alone.
The fear of people
Can do me no harm.
I live steeped in love...

26

Disgrace descends on my enchained life
And more disgrace
For my being in his power.

How did the god design my wretched fate?
The sea of nectar
Has become poison for me.

As I immerse in the depth of nectar
Death moves up to mount my heart.

Hoping for coolness if I embrace a rock,
The stone keeps melting
By the heat of my limbs.

The shade in the woodland allures me there
But the trees and the vines
Catch fire as they see me.

The flow of the *Jamunā*, instead of soothing,
Scalds me even more when I dive into it.

I must take then that poison from the sea,
How else can I end my miserable life?

16. CHIRA-HARANA (39)

17. RUKMINI SVAYAMBARAM (27, 39)

18. RUKMINI SVAYAMBARAM (27, 39)

19. KĪRTAN SINGING IN BENARES (40)

27

Who has tampered with your blue skin
And tainted your body?
Which of the devoted wives of the clan
Has squeezed you dry
Ravishing my treasure, the flavours of love?
Who has stained your mouth with lip-red
And painted you black in eye-black?...
Your forehead is pasted with vermilion powder
And your eyes are drooping in sleep.
I dare you look at my face,
I want to see you.

Are you not ashamed of yourself
To do this?
Must a woman bear so much!

28

Do not ever throw such insults, my girl!
Why can't you see by your youthful eyes
The difference between one thing and the other?
I swear by the flute that I hold in my hand:
I know of nothing else but you.
Yet still you confuse the red dust of *phāgu*,
Of the spring season rite,
With the vermilion mark of a married girl.
And the bruises from bracelets as you wrongly describe
Are nothing but scars from thorns.

29

My poor darling,
Your face seems hollow.
It hurts me to see
You adorned this way.
Your forehead, alas,
Is bruised by bracelets.
She must be wild
Who did this to you.
Your chest looks furrowed
With finger-nail scars,
Like red lotus-blooms
On a clear blue pool.
Who is that stone-girl
That harbours such ways?
Whoever taught her
This kind of loving?
It hurts me to see
Your eyes so damp.

Sit by me, darling,
I'll wipe your face clean.
You must be tired
Of the sleepless night.

30

You brought the moon down to my hands
When you used to be in love with me.
How you adored to wrap me in riches
And held me constantly on your heart.
You would not bear the empty space
That screened me from your gazing eyes.
But now it is so rare a chance
When I can have a glance at you...

31

Shame fills her world
When a girl of rank
Leaves her home
Courting death
In increasing love
With that rogue.[1]

Her soft black hair
And appearance wreck
In dust and in tears
As the night ends...

[1] Meaning Krishna.

32

I have hardened my mind
Against the name of love.
Never again shall I hear of it.
If ever I do,
I shall instantly sacrifice
This miserable life.
I have no need of love.

In markets and riverbanks
Where people gather,
They call me a whore,
Loading my world with terrible shame.

Yet still, shame cools my heart,
I feel his presence
Like the southern breeze
On the lotus-pool...

33

Bear the brunt
My wretched life,
And have your
Wishful thoughts:
That you were dead
In babyhood.
Throw overboard
The sting of pain
And amputate
The tie of love.
Since his manners
Are so unreal,
Float on scandals
And face the sea.[1]

[1] The sea of love.

34

Why did I raise those welcoming flowers
Facing my door-steps?
The bees buzz wild with the taste of honey
And his parting stings me to death.
I planted jasmine, fragrant *mālati*
And other scented blooms.
Their perfume keeps me awake at night
And I brood on the cruelty of man.

Gathering blossoms I removed their stalks
To lay a bed of petals for us.
Yet as I recline I am prickled by thorns
Without my man, my love.
And the moon shines in the clear sky,
And the birds of love sing.

Which other girl of more refinement
Has inveigled him away from me?

35

My very own man walks away to another's home
Across my courtyard,
Without even giving me a glance.
Dare I hold on to my heart and hope?
Whoever has made my Kālā[1] so changed
Let her also feel it the way as I do.
Courting such scandals
For him I have abandoned all,
Only to find his affection fade.
He is now owned by another woman.

I wish I knew how to console myself.
I dare anyone endure
The stealing of life's most precious gem.
Who has enticed my Shyām
And what spell did she cast?
Let her also burn then
The way as my life burns away.

---

[1] Kālā means black. Rādhā uses this name of Krishna to express her loving complaint.

36

I can hear the people babbling
Rādhā lives with Krishna now.
So long we lived amongst
The cowherds of *Gokula* town,
I only heard of him but never knew
Whether Krishna was black or he was white.

My husband's sister who lords our home,
Has an evil mind and a wretched tongue:
Storming my ears she welcomes a girl,
Saying, 'O, visit us, you sweetheart of Shyām'.

Who is that Shyām and whose name is Krishna
How would I know?
What is the use of making me hear it
And sneering at me?
The lord of my life alone is my goal,
I have no interest in another man.

Chandidās says that great is your bluff,
You are respectable, Rādhā.[1]

---

[1] Chandidās's comments imply that certainly the lord of Rādhā's life is not the man to whom she is married.

37

I want to forget
But I cannot forget.
I do not see him
But I am devoted to him.
Even when I sleep
I repeat his name.
When I walk in the streets
I stare at the people
And I feel like crying
If they do not mention his name...

38

What more can I tell you, my cherished one?
From life to life,[1]
In life and in death,
You are my ruling lord.
My life is bound
In a loop of love
And firmly anchored to your feet.
Having surrendered
All my care,
I am your maid to be forever free.
I have no one
In the whole of *Gokula*,
Nor on the banks of the river, *Jamunā*.
The name of Rādhā
Rouses no worry,
And I shed my tears to none.
Not a soul is there
In all the three worlds[2]
That I can call to be mine.
So calming I know
Are your lotus-feet,
I beg my shelter there...

---

[1] Refers to the conception of re-birth.
[2] Heaven, earth and the under-world. The poem depicts Rādhā's complete submission even as a maid, a state which Rādhā seldom accepts. Her love is usually mingled with pride or frustration but rarely with slavish submission. But in this particular case, Rādhā's act of tying herself to Krishna's feet expresses great devotion.

39

Do you understand
My friend, dear love,
Do you understand what it means?
No one ever thinks of me
Nor remembers my name...

40

Fear rises and fear returns
Over and over again in my heart
If Kānu[1] should flay even a grain of his love.
Villains rally to damage, destroy,
But rare is a person
Who can mend what is broken.
The more it hurts
The more I like
His calming smile;
The mead of the moon...

---

[1] Kānu is a pet name for Krishna.

41

Not knowing love
You never suffer.

My heart being dependent
My life is not free,
I am locked with a snake
In a blacked-out room.
O, loving is so hard!
I've thwarted my feelings
Revealing them to none.

Harshness at home
Hurts me like a burn,
How long can I bear
To be a girl in other's power?
The illness of love
Has been eating my heart
And now it is the remedy that kills me.

42

She lingers out of doors.
She rushes in
And she rushes out,
Her heart is restless.
Breathing fast,
She gazes at the *kadamba* wood.
What has happened
That she is not afraid?
The elders chatter
And the wicked gossip.

Is she possessed
By some enchanting god?
Forever restless
Careless of clothes,
Startled, she jumps in her dreams...

Her desire inflamed
By passion and longing,
She reaches for the moon.

Chandidās says that she is caught
In the snare of Kāliyā,[1] the dark.

---

[1] A colloquial pet name for Krishna. It refers to the episode of the subjugation by Krishna of the serpent king, Kāliya nāga.

20. KĪRTAN AUDIENCE ON THE STEPS OF THE GANGES IN BENARES (40)

21. MEETING BY THE RIVERSIDE (59)

22. TOILET OF RĀDHĀ (136)

23. ABHISĀRIKĀ (74 and note 2, p.19)

43

Like lightning in the clouds
She flashed away.
Her friends shadowing her
Melted in the space.
Never have I seen a girl as this:
Like patches of wild colour
Her ways were playful,
Eyes abyss deep.
Round her neck swayed a string of pearls.
Enchanted bees hummed at her fragrant skin.
Revealing and hiding her beautiful form
She walked away
Arm in arm with her friends.
Smiling a glance and looting my heart
She walked away.
Moonlight exploded on her glazed finger nails.
Her fatal eyes collected massacred lovers.
I lay unconscious with wounded heart,
My ribs cut open by her stabbing glance.

Chandidās says:
It is an absorbing tale
Of an illness that does not end in the grave!

44

He was black,
He had poison-eyes.
A glance from him brought death to my side,
Life lay open to love's five arrows.[1]
Nothing else mattered—
Food or rest.
I disowned all decorative dress.
My heart raced for the *kadamba* wood.
Having abandoned
Fear and shame,
Like a wild woman I begged for the jewel.[2]

---

[1] Five arrows of Madan, the god of love.
[2] The jewel or *ratan* represents love. Often love is described as *piriti-ratan*, the love-jewel.

45

If, by a great chance, love should ever shoot forth, you must watch the sprout day and night and water it with tears. If, with luck and care, you find signs of leaves on it, wait by it and hope that it will grow into a vine. This is the vine of adoration that binds two hearts in one intimate bond, driving away the fear of social customs and gossip.

With the growing adoration, desire increases between the two, bringing forth flower buds to the vine. Two such hearts, both conscious and continuously devoted to loving, are found once in a million. I have no doubt that the ultimate flowering of the plant depends on the awareness of love.

46

It's no use telling me what I should do,
The blackness of his skin fills my days and my dreams.
I can't even move my hand to fix my tousled tresses.
Taking them for Krishna I fill my lap with my hair.
As I call out for him, my dark darling Kālā,[1]
I cry and cry.
My black hair is left in a loose knot now.
When Kālā my black one comes to my mind
I let my hair down and brood over it.
The blackness of his skin is forever present,
What can I do?

---

[1] Kālā is another name for Krishna. The hair is often considered a symbol of sex and its blackness is related to Krishna's complexion.

47

What may I call this,
My friend?
Such were his promises
That life is not worth living.
He has no faith nor fear,
Only a bandit is he.
But I know my fate
Is to love a bandit...

48

Whatever the elders at home may say
I can never leave my treasure, my Shyām,
His beauty and charm have eaten my heart.
I constantly fear that someone will come
And cut my ribs open to take them away.
Forever I am conscious, awake day and night,
Even when in lassitude I close my eyes.
I am buried in Shyām, the shape of my loves.

Who could ever wish me to leave my loving,
I would rather eat poison than hear such words.
I have explored his beauty and found no shores,
But the god at last is standing by me.
I will fulfill my dream and let the rest go.

49

What have I gained
Saying Krishna and Krishna.
My heart is bruised raw,
Life simply sizzles
And I am dying of the fire of my mind.
In Gokula the town of the cowherds,
Nothing is forbidden!
They act as they wish.
The girls full of youth
Are ladies of homes.
Only Rādhā is the scandalous one!

Since the cruel god that created love
Made it dependent on the other's response,
I have no wish to live.
And I beg you not to name a girl Rādhā again.

50

My mouth is silent
For the word 'love'.
My love of Shyām
Is the sadness of life...

51

Someone in love can know my feelings.
Chatterings of neighbours
Leave me untouched,
My heart, obsessed, races at him.
I am working at home
And am choking in silence,
Never can I cry for my love aloud.
There is no one in the world
Who can bring me some comfort,
I am worried like a woman
Who is wedded to a thief...

52

Sit yourself down for a while,
My friend,
I wish to talk about that flute[1] of Shyām.
It robbed me in broad daylight
Of everything I owned.
It wounded my heart
And set fire to my life,
But I would not know why.
Nothing can I think of again,
My heart has no rest.
That flute has been deafening me...

---

[1] The flute of Krishna has been a constant source of suffering and enchantment for Rādhā.

53

Let us not talk of that fatal flute.
It calls a woman away from her home
And drags her by the hair to that Shyām.
A devoted wife forgets her spouse
To be drawn like a deer, thirsty and lost.
Even the wisest of ascetics lose their minds
And the plants and the trees delight in its sound.
What then can a helpless innocent girl do?

54

Has Rādhā pain in her heart?
She lingers alone in a desolate state
Heedless to all.
Her reflective gaze
Is fixed on the clouds,
She has no taste for food,
Nor for dress.
She is attired as a *yogini*[1]
Disowning the world.
Her plaited hair
Is adorned with flowers
But she lets it down
To brood on it.
Smiling she gazes
Again at the clouds
And whispers, longingly
Raising her arms.
Her eyes focus
On the twining necks
Of peacocks in love.[2]

Chandidās says:
This is the dawn of love
For Rādhā and her dark beloved.

---

[1] A woman who has renounced the world for spiritual reasons.
[2] Rādhā's black hair and the black clouds represent Krishna, the dark one. The loving peacocks symbolize the months of the rains, the season of fertility and love.

55

Cloud-coloured Kānu,[1] dark mascara,
Kānu, all nectar, has at last appeared!
My eyes, like the bird that thirsts for the moon,
Cannot bear the delay of an eyelid's flutter.
I saw Shyām's[2] beauty going to the stream.
Garlands of flowers swing from his neck,
Bees hum about that Idol of Delight.
His glances remove all memory of the world.
Those eyes, like the arrows of the god of love,
Raid my life, pierce my heart,
Killing my sense of right and wrong.
And they draw me body and soul.

[1, 2] Kānu and Shyām, among many others, are also Krishna's names.

56

The night was dense,
Clouds assembled,
But, how did he come?
In my courtyard
Standing in the rains
He was soaking and breaking my heart.
O friend, I cannot describe
What luck brought me my love
To my own doorstep.
My home was filled
With heartless elders,
I was delayed and worried.
I made signs at him
Only to hurt.
His love made me feel
Proud of all blame.
He suffered joyfully
But my sadness he shared...

57

I must go.
In spite of my kisses,
My passionate embraces,
He keeps repeating
That he must go.
He goes half a step
And then he turns back
With anguished eyes,
Gazing at my face.

Wringing my hands
He promises returning
He flatters me so much
To meet me again!
Deep is his love,
My beloved one,
Of such terrible passion.

Chandidās says: then
Rest in his heart.

58

The morning crows and the *kokila*[1] cried
The end of the night.
My lover was up and hastily left
Fixing his dishevelled hair.
I cannot describe my suffering, O friend!
My dark lover left me saying not a word,
My heart was aching.
Resting in lassitude
My eyes were heavy,
As I discovered his clothes on me.

My people at home are eager to blame,
What can I do with his dress on me?

Chandidās says with a joyful heart,
Suffering leads to the treasures of love.

---

[1] The Indian cuckoo, the bird of spring and love.

24. RĀDHĀ AT KRISHNA'S FEET (92)

25. HE WAS BLACK, HE HAD POISON-EYES! (98)

59

It's all my fault,
My sweet,
It's all my fault.
Whom can I blame for my falling in love
As an innocent fool?
The ocean of nectar that filled me with joy
Was only poison when I drank it.
I was sad and sad
But how would I know?

My caste and my home
Are all destroyed,
My hopes and trust are dead.
You do not love me as before
But I long to see you.

60

...Love was the sea of joy
When I went in.
I rushed out shivering
As the wind blew sorrow ashore.
The sea of love was crystal clear
But for the alligator sorrow,
My life was a quivering drop.

Elders stagnate like water-moss,
Neighbours are spiky fish,
Fruits of thorn float in my sea,
The water-weeds sting.
I am burnt in my skin and heart.
The gift of sorrow
Mingles my joy.

    Says Chandidās:
    The joy and the sorrow
    Are brothers born together.
    If you love for joy,
    Sorrow must enter your home.[1]

---

[1] The importance of sorrow is a great theme in Chandidās's songs. He treats sorrow as the exact counterpart of joy.

61

With care I combed the earth
And I found the seed of love.
As I planted it,
It grew into a tree
Blossoming my death.
Why did the tree of love grow?
Now I spend my unfortunate life,
My days and my nights,
Watering the plant.
I had heard of happiness in love.

I bought poison for nectar
And ate my own joy.
My mouth burns with the taste
But I learnt Krishna's ways.
My wish is fulfilled
And I need no longer love.

Chandidās enquires
Can you bear your limbs
Untouched by him?

DWIJA CHANDIDĀS

62

My growing youth is my one great danger
And then,
The dreaded forest of Brindā,
The *kadamba* grove,
The flowing Jamunā,
My beautiful jewels,
Mount Gobardhan,
And with all these dangers I live alone
With no one to share my tales.

63

O friend, who made me hear the name of Shyām?
Through the ears, piercing my heart,
It threw my life into confusion.
Such honey in the name of Shyām,
My tongue can never leave it:
Tasting it over and over again,
I have lost control.
How shall I reach him?

If such is the power of his name,
What would happen if I touched his body?
How could a young girl keep to the right path
Knowing where he lives.
O, how I want to avoid such thoughts,
Such stubborn thoughts, I cannot escape.
What shall I do?

A chaste girl wrecks her chastity
Assaying her own youth, says Dwija Chandidās.

64

Consuming me, she moved away,
The golden goddess.
The glow of her skin ripped open her sari
As her form fought with the azure blue dress.
How would I hold
The lightning in my eyes?—
I could no longer watch.

Her eyes were restless,
Bracelets jingled.
The bees flew drunk with the flavour of her fragrance,
And she walked away like an elegant swan.
Her hips were firm as the pride of a lioness
But blending with the sweetness of honey.
What nectar glistened in her smiling eyes!

65

...Can anyone follow
the ways of my pain?
I live on the edge of a razor
that cuts me to shreds
as I move...

66

Beloved barefaced one,
Do you not sense any feeling of shame
Visiting others in the morning?
Your chest displays a cicatrice
From armlet attacks.

Which of the stars in the art of loving
Got hold of you?—
That your nails are painted with blood
And your forehead is scarred
By cinnabar mark[1]
And black mascara darkens your lips?

Dearest, I am dazzled by the splendour
Of it all,
But for your eyes
That still suppress tears
In memory of the parting
From your beautiful love.

---

[1] The vermilion powder is used by a married woman on her forehead and the parting of her hair as signs of love and fulfilment in marriage. These words show that Krishna was engaged in sexual union with a married woman.

67

Black poison burns me.
A dumb woman,
Married,
I live in a respectable home.
My heart wrapped in pain,
Speechlessly,
Secretly, chokes
As the flute grates my ears.
It lures my senses away
Leaving me my corpse.
It has no feeling for right or wrong.
The straight born reed
On the lips of that rogue[1]
Has learned to be crooked.

Says Dwija Chandidās:
The company is wrong.
In the teeth of Rāhu[2]
The moon too turns black.

---

[1] Krishna.
[2] Rāhu is the evil force that devours the moon during lunar eclipse.

68

...My heart can no longer rest
In the household work.
My days and my nights are filled with tears
But scandals make me laugh.

O, the pitiless flute!
It forced me give my youth
To Shyām
Turning me into his slave.
I felt like a beggar for love.

Straight outside,
The reed is hollow to the core.
Sipping the nectar of his lips
It vomits only venom.
If ever I could reach
Where the reeds grew,
I would pull them out
Roots, stalks and all.
And throw them into the sea.

Says Dwija Chandidās:
What can the poor reed do?
Can you resist Krishna
Who is at the roots?

69

Enough of this country for me,
I must go to a distant land.
I cannot hear of this absurd love
Nor can I see any lovers...

70

Who brought into the world
The name of love?
Ashes for sugar,
Bitterness of body.
Friend, there is nothing I can say
Inscrutably the word
Dwells in my heart.
The love of my lover
Is my own desire
That keeps on growing
And can never end.
Like callous Death
He toys with love,
Forcing my passion
Till it rivals death.
Chatter of neighbours
Floods my world with shame
And still my longing
Swells and swells.
I bear and bear it like the earth.
Love soaks my body.
On love I dote,
Bearing it as I can.
Love makes me mad.
I do not know
The ways of love
Nor where they go.

Says Dwija Chandidās:
Great love is only grief.[1]

---

[1] Translated by Deben Bhattacharya in collaboration with W. G. Archer.

26. KRISHNA SAYING FAREWELL TO RĀDHĀ (III)

27. KRISHNA LEAVING RĀDHĀ IN HASTE FORGETTING HIS SHAWL (112)

BADU CHANDIDĀS

71

Tell me,
Tell me my beautiful love,
Why do your limbs appear numb,
Lips tremble
And eyes well up with tears?
Shivers surrounding your delicate frame
Choke your life
As you silently brood,
Gazing at nothing.
What do you think
And what do you see?

Says Badu Chandidās:
I know for sure,
The flute has entered her ears.

72

Darkness and clouds
Shroud the frightening night,
Alone, I suffer
Under the *kadamba* tree.
I scan distances in vain,
Krishna is nowhere.
Split the earth open
And I will conceal myself.
My youth runs away,
Yet still my heart suffocates
Waiting for Krishna...

73

The cries of the black *kokila*
Blackens Brindāvan
Like the forest of death.
The other hazard
Is the son of Nanda.
My life hungers
For the sound of his reed-flute...

74

Who plays the flute on the Jamunā bank?
Who plays the flute on the pastoral land
of Gokula, the city of the cowherds—
driving my body to desperate longing
and filling my mind with restlessness?
In utter confusion is my household work
for the music of that flute.
Who plays the flute?
Who is he?...

75

I have no idea
What made me lose my heart to Krishna,
This terrible love chokes me to death.
My world is intolerable
With rising heat,
My heart is stung
By a venomous snake.

Casting away
All ethics of castes
My heart dotes on Krishna
Day and night.
The custom of the clan
Is a far-away cry
And now I know
That love adheres wholly
To its own laws.

76

Like the rise of the new sun
Through water-laden clouds,
The red mark of cinnabar[1]
Shines on her hair.
Her fair face glowing
As a lotus of gold
Shamed the moon
And made him run away
Two million miles...

[1] See note on page 123.

77

The first watch of the night was a world of a lovely dream!
Under the *kadamba* tree Kānu[1] held me to his side,
Kissed my lotus-like face.
Painting me with sandal paste, gently he spoke to me
And sweetly played on his bamboo flute.
He wanted to make love to me,
But I did not let him.
I was still dreaming till the second watch.

At the third watch of the night I was clasped to his heart,
Still gazing at his moon-like face.
Smiling, he stole my heart away,
I was anxious and restless for love.
At the fourth watch of the night Kānu drank my lips,
And I longed to be loved.

Sings Badu Chandidās:
Suddenly a cruel scream from the morning *kokila* bird
Shattered my sleep and dream.

---

[1] Kānu is a pet name for Krishna.

78

Krishna,
You must understand the nature of a woman,
And not be in a rage.
As you could see,
My anger faded
The moment you spoke.

The god of passion
Has linked into one
Your heart and mine,
Moulding our love
Into one unique life,
In one single frame...

I must ask you for something,
Krishna,
You won't have our ways
With another girl[1]
Will you, my love?

---

[1] Even though Rādhā was accustomed to Krishna's fickleness, her desire to protect that particular spirit, that unique feeling, which grew in her through the love between herself and Krishna, reflects a universal pattern.

A parallel could be drawn from *A Farewell to Arms* by Ernest Hemingway. Towards the end of the book, Catherine, on her death bed, makes a similar request even though she wishes her husband to have girls after her death. In one of the most moving sentences of the book she asks: 'You won't do our things with another girl, or say the same things, will you?' Catherine was haunted by the fear that what she treated as sacred might turn profane.

79

The rounded *kadambas* in full bloom
Weigh down the boughs,
Yet Gopāla[1] is still not here
In Gokula.
How long can I conceal in silk
My breasts?[2]
Who could have disarrayed
Our childhood bond?
Krishna of cruel heart silently left
And never returned.

I will wipe out my red mark of love,[3]
Smash my bangles to smithereens.
Like a doe stabbed by a poison-dart,
My life burns away...
Remembering Krishna day and night,
My heart houses a thunderbolt.
The month of *Jaistha*[4] came and went,
The month of *Āsārh* is here now.
With the southern sky overcast
By dark cumulus cloud,
There is still no sign
Of the cruel boy.

---

[1] Another of Krishna's various names, representing him as a cowherd.

[2] The use of the *kadamba* bloom image in the beginning of the poem is to establish the roundness and the golden complexion of Rādhā's breasts.

[3] The vermilion mark on the parting of the hair of a woman indicates marriage. But Rādhā, never having been married to Krishna, was unable to use this conventional sign. The poet uses this symbolism to suggest that their bond was as firm as that of conventional marriage.

[4] *Jaistha*, from the middle of May to the middle of June and *Āsārh* is the month that follows *Jaistha*.

80

It is in the month of *Āsārh*[1]
As the new clouds roar,
My eyes pour over the tyranny of love.
And I have no wings—
Or else I would have flown
Where Krishna, my life's lord, lives.
How can I survive four long months
Of torrential rain?
Kānu has let down
My laden youth.

It is in the month of *Shrāvana*,[2]
Again and again
As the rains fall,
Bearing unbearable pain
From love's flower-arrows;
Sleepless, I lie in my lonely bed...

It is in the month of *Bhādar*
As darkness veils the day
And the peacock
And the *dāhuk*[3]
And the bullfrog
Cry
Their suggestive clamours,
Brooding, brooding,
Missing his face,
My heart explodes.

It is in the month of *Āshin*
As the rains stall
And the cloud crawls away
And the reed-spray blossoms,
My life seems buried
In failure
With Krishna being away.

[1] *Āsārh* is the opening month of the rains, from the middle of June to the middle of July.
[2] *Shrāvan*, *Bhādar* and *Āshin* are the months that follow *Āsārh*. Apart from the traditional springtime associations as observed the world over, India has a second season for love, the monsoon period.
[3] The bird *dāhuk* which usually lives in the river areas of Bengal, mates in the monsoon season.

SAHAJA POEMS

81

How can I describe
what is love
and when it is born
and where it is seen
and who found it
and how?

A connoisseur
draws out love
with tender care
from the pulsation of leaves,
from the rays of the flowers...

82

Using one's body
As a medium of prayer
And loving spontaneously
Is the *Sahaja* love...

28. RĀDHĀ AND KRISHNA IN EACH OTHER'S CLOTHES (112)

29. I SCAN DISTANCES IN VAIN (132)

83

They all chatter
Of *Sahaja* love
But who can discern
What *Sahaja* means?
One who has gone
Beyond the depth
Of darkness[1] knows.

Like moon-girls
Haloing the moon,
The girls of *Gokula*
Close in on Krishna.
Poison and nectar
In an act of love.

This is the perfume of love,
Can you understand it?...

[1] Unconsciousness.

84

God is the only way.
If god leaves
Strength leaves.
If god goes
Body goes...

85

It is annoying to find people aspiring to practise *Sahaja*, or even thinking of it, without knowing its inner meaning and its spiritual implications.

Their behaviour resembles that of the crow trying to imitate the nightingale, and of the glow-worm that twinkles a million times hoping to equal the moon, and of the monkey that reaches for the heavenly *pārijāt* which is a rare flower even for the gods...

86

The changeless land,
heaven, is the home
of a *Sahaja* man.
But, then how
does he enter the heart?...

87

Looking deep
Into the well of feelings,
See how
Bodies dissolve
In one single form.
And all seeds
Needing to be born,
Unite in one
For one great revelation:
Love...

88

The essence of love
Is the only cause
For being
A lover and being loved.
And body
Is the birth place
Of the essence of love.
A beloved is born
For the sake of the lover
And for both of them
The passion-play...

89

Kāma,
The great goddess of love,
And Madana,
Her lord,
Represent the divine
Feminine energy
And
The supreme masculine force.
The spontaneous[1] man
Is as old and wise
As the father of their fathers.

Nothing is far away,
Everything is near:
The Universe
And the painting on the wall...

[1] *Sahaja* man.

90

Mastering *Sahaja* love is a great art. It implies the ability to extend one's person to the very limits of space—east and west, north and south, all directions having an immediate and simultaneous meaning.

To extract happiness from *Sahaja* love, it must be treated as a deep secret yet the wishes must be fulfilled. It is as difficult as making a frog dance in the mouth of a snake which is not allowed to eat the frog. It is like dangling a mountain with a cotton thread, like imprisoning an elephant in a cobweb...

91

One who pervades
the great Universe
is seen by none
unless a man knows
the unfolding
of love...

On the earth
rests the water,
on water
rest the waves
and on waves
afloat is love...

Love, love and love.
This four-letter word
carries a multiple
of opinions.
But if you adore it
and go deeper and deeper,
you will find that
it is the only One—
Wholly love.

92

Find your match
In a worthy love
Before you lose your heart.
Love is a jewel
To be guarded with care
When lovers are equal
In maturity...

93

Like the tongue flirting with the tooth
Suffers sharp pain at the slightest bite,
A good girl adoring an evil boor
Gains a body-load of viperous stings...

94

My body corrodes
And my heart grows heavy
Since I heard of *Sahaja* love.
I was so very young.

When the god wills
And I meet my love,
My honours and virtues
And my prides and patience,
The laws of the Vedas[1]
Will totally erupt.

I have thrown in the river
The care of my caste,
Leaving my husband.
I have demolished
All religious rites,
My errors and guilts...

---

[1] The Vedas are the earliest available sacred texts of India.

95

Sun rays
Streaming down on the water
Make it rise.
The fire of loving
Sizzles the heart
To raise it high
As the lion-man
And the lotus-girl[1]
Engage in a worship...

---

[1] *Padmini* is described as the most desirable type of woman in the *Kāmasutra* of Vātsyāyana which is considered to have been written between the first and the fourth century. Her sexual organ is said to resemble a budding lotus. *Padma* means lotus.

96

Away from the contact
Of all stains,
The seeker
Dwells in the lake of love,
With purity
As his sole companion.

Pollution tends to make
Its rendezvous in hell...

97

Who could master
The leading emotion
Held in the flavour of love?[1]
Only he who
Wholly knows
The soul of the mood,
Should worship
The spirit of loving.
Love is the essence
Of all emotions,[2]
Krishna and Rādhā
Its body and soul.
A lover-devotee
Dissolves in that love...

[1] *Shringāra rasa.* A rasa represents the aesthetic and spiritual as well as the physical flavours experienced when expressing an emotion. It is much more than a mood, or a state of mind since it evokes a feeling of exaltation in the successful experience of a *rasa. Shringāra* is love.

[2] According to the classical theory of drama, there are nine *rasas* or dramatic moods. These are *Shringāra* (love), *Hāsya* (laughter), *Karuna* (pathos), *Vīra* (heroism), *Raudra* (wrath), *Bhayānaka* (fear), *Vībhatsa* (disgust), *Adbhuta* (wonder) and *Shānta* (peace).

98

Give up your pride
O proud, lovable girl,
Your riches can never be
Ever-lasting.
If compassion
Is lacking in you
And I take poison,
You will bear
The guilt of my death.
But I will be born again
To slave for you...

30. THE FIRST WATCH OF THE NIGHT (137)

31. THE PASSION-PLAY (150)

99

Beloved,
It hurts me
To let secrets out.
With you and me
And our love between us,
We are transformed
Into Rādhā and Krishna,
All into one.

Passion rises
From the natural joy
Born in the heart.

We are all one
With the eternal love
That dwells
In *Braja*[1]...

---

[1] The region of *Braja* is that area surrounding Gokula, Govardhan, Brindāvan and Mathurā etc., where Krishna spent his youth.

100

Youthful girls,
Those imbued
With love for you
Are pure
As the pupils
Of my eyes.
I can even smear
The face of the god
With
Black shame
For creating love
Only to lead it
To a tragic end...

I do not wish
To see those faces
With mouths
That have never plunged into mouths.
I have no time
For men who are born
In this living world
But dead to love.[1]

---

[1] A similar *Sahaja* reference can be found in some of the poems by Vidyāpati who was born in Mithila in AD 1352. For example:

> Lend your ears
> To these profitable words,
> O beautiful girl,
> Great is the virtue
> Of serving others.
> She who never encounters
> Rapture outside marriage,
> May her face stay
> Away from my path
> As I start the day.
> A girl who is unaware of
> The happiness of love
> With at least five men*
> Is as unholy
> As an evil spirit.
>
> Says Vidyāpati:
> Listen, my girl of great merit,

101

There are three categories of men: the customary, the un-organic and the spontaneous.[1]

The customary man is the embodiment of flesh and blood, cultivated by his actions, habits and destiny. Springing from the primordial waters of heaven, he moves continuously and unconsciously between life and death.

The un-organic man dwells in heaven, the changeless land, as a ray of love, forever united with the lord of heaven.

But even above heaven is the Forest of Brinda,[2] the land of Eternity, which is open to the *Sahajiyā*,[3] the spontaneous man.

A woman of one husband
Knows nothing of love.

Quoted in *Chandidāser Padāvali*, by Shri Bimanbihari Mazumdar, Calcutta, 1960. Translated by Deben Bhattacharya.

* Obviously this reference is made to Draupadi (of the Indian epic *Mahābhārata*) who was married to the five Pandu brothers—Yudhisthira, Bhīma, Arjuna, Nakula and Sahadeva—at the suggestion of their mother Kunti. To the Hindus, Draupadi represents one of the supreme examples of chaste womanhood, in the same way that virginity of the mother of Christ is exemplified to Christians by divine decree.

[1] *Sahaja*.
[2] *Brindāvan*, the place of Krishna's youthful days and loves. According to the *Sahaja* interpretation, the heavenly world is divided into three parts: *Golak*, *Vaikuntha* and *Brindāvan*. *Vaikuntha* is the domain of *Vishnu*, the preserving god of the Hindu Triple-Force. *Golak* is the sphere of cowherds representing Krishna's childhood period.
[3] *Sahajiyā* means one who follows the *Sahaja* path.

102

All go chattering
Man, man, man,
The word
That hides the deepest of thoughts.
Man is a resident
Of the greatest height,
Above and beyond
Everything else.
If you should know
Who is housed
In the depth
Of the deep, deep sea of love,
The nature of man
Might reveal itself.
The laws of the Vedas[1]
And the wisdom of Vishnu[2]
Throw no light
On the substance called man.
Man is unique
And a joy to the universe.

---

[1] The four Vedas—*Rig, Yajur, Sāma* and *Atharva*—are the earliest known scriptures related to the origin of religious and philosophical thoughts of India.

[2] Vishnu is the preserving god of the Hindu Triple-Force, the other two being Brahmā, indicating the creative, and Shiva the dissolving forces. Krishna is a reincarnation of Vishnu.

103

Who can know
The creation—woman?
Even the god
Who brought her into being
Has no clue at all.
Poison and nectar
Were blended into one.

The lamp that throws light,
Holds a flame in her heart
And the loving moth
Wanders to his fiery death.
A man can march
To his funeral, in lust.
But a lover drinks the nectar
Sieving poison out...

104

The most difficult of all words
is the *man*:
Man that embodies
all faith and its ways,
action with its continuous
chain of effects.[1]
Man is the greatest of all.

Who then is the man?
Rising against the man-made rules
when laws of love are threatened,
man is the connoisseur
of the ethos of love...[2]

And all who keep claiming
to be connoisseurs of love,
are far from it.
Only one in a million
knows the essence of feelings.

[1] *Karma.*   [2] *Rasika.*

105

The essence of beauty
springs
from the eternal play
of man as Krishna
and woman as Rādhā.
Devoted lovers
in the act of loving,
seek to reach
the goal.
Who is devoted
to whom and how
is of no interest.
Dedicate your soul
to the service of loving.[1]
Love was born
to Rādhā
as one by one,
her eight friends[2] helped.
If your senses
and the mind
can grasp the essence,
Krishna is reached.

Says Chandidās:
Listen, O, brother man,
Man is the greatest Truth
Of all,
Nothing beyond.

---

[1] *'Munjari'*, a particular sect among the Vaishnavas, approach Krishna through *Munjari* way. In this, the human emotions are translated into the devotion to Krishna through his service. The devotee concentrates on Rādhā, serving her and assisting her in her union with Krishna.

[2] *'Astasakhi'*; Rādhā's eight women friends, Lalitā, Vishākhā, Champakalatā, Chitrā, Tungavidyā, Indulekhā, Rangadevi and Sudevi, who often assisted her when she was in any difficulty with Krishna.

All this section of the poem is written in the form of a numerical riddle, probably in order to keep the text understandable only to an initiate in the *Sahaja* ways. For instance, Rādhā's friends are referred to only by the number eight and Krishna by number one since *'ka'* is the first letter of the Bengali alphabet.

BIBLIOGRAPHY

Bengali

Ayub, Abu Said and Mukhopadhyay, Hirendranath, (ed.) *Ādhunik Bānglā Kabitā*, Calcutta, 1940.

Bandyopadhay, Saroj, (ed.) *Vaishnava Padaratnāvali*, Calcutta, 1961.

Basumati Sāhitya Mandir, (Publishers), *Vaishnava Mahājan Padāvali*, Calcutta, no date.

Basu, Shankariprasad, *Chandidās O Vidyāpati*, Calcutta, 1960.

Bhattacharya, Byomakesh, *Mirābāi*, Varanasi, 1957.

Bhattacharya, Upendranath, *Bānglār Bāul O Bāul Gān*, Calcutta, 1957.

Lahiri, Durgadas, *Vaishnava Padalaharī*, Calcutta, 1905.

Mazumdar, Bimanbihari, *Chandidāser Padāvali*, Calcutta, 1960.

Pānchshata Batsarer Padāvali, Calcutta, 1961.

Shodash shatābdir Padāvali-Sāhitya, Calcutta, 1961.

Mukhopadhyay, Harekrishna, *Vaishnava Padāvali*, Calcutta, 1961.

Rāy, Kalidas, *Padāvali Sāhitya*, Calcutta, 1961.

Prāchin Banga Sāhitya, Calcutta, no date.

Sahana, Satyakinkar, *Chandidās-Prasanga*, Calcutta, 1959.

English

Archer, W. G., *The Loves of Krishna*, London, 1957.

(ed.) *The Kama Sutra*, translated by Sir Richard Burton and F. F. Arbuthnot, London, 1963.

Bazar Paintings of Calcutta, London, 1953.

Aurobindo, Sri, (transl.) *Songs of Vidyāpati*, Pondicherry, 1956.

Bhattacharya, Deben, (transl.) *Love Songs of Vidyāpati*, ed. W. G. Archer, London, 1963.

Coomaraswamy, A. C., 'Sahaja', *The Dance of Shiva*, New York, 1957.

Hoffmann, Helmut, *The Religions of Tibet*, London, 1961.

Keyt, G., (transl.) *Sri Jayadeva's Gīta Govinda*, Bombay, 1947.

Nicholson, R. A., *RUMI—Poet and Mystic*, London, 1956.

Sen, Dinesh Chandra, *History of Bengali Language and Literature*, Calcutta, 1911.

DISCOGRAPHY

BAM LD 014: Musique Traditionelle de l'Inde, La Boite à Musique, Paris.
BAM LD 015: Musique Religieuse de l'Inde, La Boite à Musique, Paris.
v.41: Rhythmes et Melodies du Bengale, Club Français du Disque, Paris.
FE 4431: Religious Music of India, Folkways, New York.
ALP 1855: Shyama—Tagore Centenary, 1961. His Master's Voice, London.
EALP 1256: Voice of Tagore, H.M.V., Dum Dum, India.
ECLP 2256: Folk Songs of Bengal, H.M.V., Dum Dum, India.
ALPC 2: Morning and Evening Ragas, His Master's Voice, London.
ALPC 7: Music of India, His Master's Voice, London.
8155 RL: Music from India, Philips, Baarn, Holland.

The author has published a record one side of which (21 minutes) is devoted to the following songs from the present volume:

1. *O friend, who made me hear the name of Shyām* (page 120)
2. *It is a disgrace* (page 41)

including impromptu commentary on the songs by Shri Nabagopal Mitra-Thakur, one of the greatest singers of Chandidās's songs.

This record with sleeve notes in English and French bears the following title:

'RELIGIOUS SONGS FROM BENGAL—*Songs of the Bāuls and Poems of Chandidās*', recorded in India, edited by Deben Bhattacharya, No. LD 099, Editions de la Boîte à Musique, 133 Boulevard Raspail, Paris 6eme. Distributed in New York by Record and Tape Sales Corporation.

INDEX

Ādi, 9
Aishvarya, 40
Arjuna, 38
Āsārh, 139, 140
Āshin, 140
Āyāna, 39

Badu, 9
Badu Chandidās, 10, 38, 49, 129, 131, 137
Bakula, 17, 24
Bali, 29, and illustration No. 5
Bankura, 10
Bāshuli, 18, 19, 25, 26
Bhādar, 140
Bhagavad-Gitā, 38
Bhāgavata Purāna, 39
Bhakti, 40
Bhrigu, 29
Birbhum, 10, 17, 27, 33, and illustration Nos. 2, 3
Bishnu Day, 35
Brahma, 37
Brahmā, 38
Brahmadaitya, 26
Brāhmana, 10, 18, 21, 22, 24-6, 50
Braja, 2, 161
Brindā, 119, 163
Brindāvan, 33, 41, 44, 133
Buddha, 29, 48, and illustration No. 6
Buddhism, 47, 49, 50

Chaitanya, 39, 40, 42
Chandidās, 9, 10, 17-27, 31-3, 35, 37, 38, 40, 41, 44, 47, 49, 50, 53, 90, 96, 97, 108, 111, 112, 114, 115, 167
Chhāndogya Upanishad, 38
Chhatna, 10

Dāhuk, 140
Dashāvatāra-stotra, 28
Devabhāshā, 28
Dhrupad, 42
Dīn, 10
Dīn Chandidās, 50
Domni, 50
Dwija, 10
Dwija Chandidās, 10, 17, 38, 42, 49, 117, 120, 124, 125, 127

Gad khemtā, 42
Gīta Govinda, 27, 28, 30, 31, 48
Gitanjali, 27
Gobardhan, 119
Gokula, 90, 92, 103, 134, 139, 145
Gopāla, 139
Govindadās, 9, 33, 34
Gurjari, 30

Haladhara, 29
Hiranyakashipu, 29, and illustration No. 4

Islam, 49, 50

Jaistha, 139
Jalalu'l Dīn Rūmī, 49
Jamunā, 29, 44, 80, 92, 119, 134
Jayadeva, 27, 28, 30-3, 48
Jesus, 37
Jnānadās, 34

Kabir, 33
Kadamba, 56, 62, 96, 98, 119, 132, 137, 139
Kalki, 30
Kālā, 38, 89, 100
Kāliyā, 38, 96
Kāma, 151
Kamsa, 41
Kāna, 34
Kānu, 38, 94, 109, 137, 140
Kathakali, 27, and illustration Nos. 17, 18
Khemtā, 42
Khol, 40, 41
Kīrtan, 17, 26, 40-2, and illustration Nos. 19, 20
Kokila, 30, 66, 112, 133, 137
Krishna, 17, 19-21, 26-8, 30-5, 38-41, 43-6, 48-50, 60, 62, 64, 70-2, 74, 90, 100, 103, 115, 125, 132, 135, 138-40, 145, 159, 161, 167, and illustration Nos. 11, 12, 15, 24, 26-8
Kshatriya, 29, 50
Kubjā, 33, 34, 41, 42

Madana, 151
Mādhava, 34
Mādhurya, 40

171

Mādhvāchārya, 39
Mahābhārata, 38, 39
Mālati, 88
Mālava Gauda, 30
Māthur, 41, 42
Mathura, 33, 41, 42, 44
Megha Malhāra, 30
Mīrābāi, 30, 33
Mlechchhas, 30
Moksha, 40
Muslims, 48, 49

Nakul, 21–4
Nanda, 77, 133
Nannur, 10, 19
Nimbārka, 39
Nirvāna, 40

Odantapura, 48

Pālā, 40–2
Pal kings, 47, 48
Parakīyā, 50
Pārijāt, 147
Phāgu, 82

Rādhā, 17, 20, 21, 23, 26, 27, 30–4, 38–42, 44, 46, 48–50, 90, 92, 103, 108, 159, 161, 167, and illustration Nos. 22, 24, 26–8
Raga, 30, and illustration No. 8
Rāhu, 124
Rāi, 34, 38, 42
Rāma, 29
Rāmakrishna, 37
Rāmānujāchārya, 39
Rāmi, 9, 18–26
Rāmini, 9, 20
Rāvana, 29
Rukmini, 39, and illustration Nos. 17, 18

Sahaja, 9, 19, 20, 38, 39, 44–51, 141, 144, 145, 147, 148, 152, 156
Sahajayāna, 47, 48, 50
Sahajiyā, 51, 163
Sant Tukārām, 33
Sen, Dinesh Chandra, 26
Sen kings, 48, 50
Sen, Samar, 37
Shakti, 25
Shiva, 38
Shrāvana, 30, 140
Shudras, 50
Shyām, 38, 42, 63, 74, 89, 90, 102, 104, 106, 107, 109, 120, 125
Sudāmā, 40
Sufism, 49
Surdās, 33

Tagore, Rabindranath, 9, 27
Tāntrik religion, 47
Trishakti, 38

Vaishnava, 30, 33, 35, 36, 38, 39, 48
Vaishnavas, 38, 48
Vaishyas, 50
Vallabhāchārya, 39
Vāmana (Dwarf), 29, and illustration No. 5
Vasanta, Raga, 30, and illustration No. 8
Vedas, 28, 156, 164
Vidyāpati, 31–3
Vikramashila, 48
Vishnu, 25, 28, 38, 48, 164
Vrishabhānu, 39

Yashodā, 39, 40
Yoga, 45
Yogini, 108

UNESCO Collection of Representative Works Indian Series.

This book has been accepted in the Indian Series of the Translations Collection of UNESCO.

© UNESCO 1967, 1969

First published by George Allen & Unwin Ltd., London, 1967.

For Product Safety Concerns and Information please contact our EU
representative GPSR@taylorandfrancis.com
Taylor & Francis Verlag GmbH, Kaufingerstraße 24, 80331 München, Germany

www.ingramcontent.com/pod-product-compliance
Lightning Source LLC
Chambersburg PA
CBHW061446300426
44114CB00014B/1865